M000222285

YOUR SELF-SABOTAGING INNER BULLY:

Standing Up to It Once and For All!

By:
Dr. Sidney J Cohen Ph.D.

Table of Contents

DEDICATION

This book is dedicated to the number one source of my professional inspiration over my years in practice: *my patients.* So many of you mustered up the courage to do the ongoing work required to get control over your clinical symptoms—and personally grow as a human being in the process. For those of you who on your own continue to do that work, my respect for your efforts is huge indeed. Please know too it has been my honor to try to help you out in any way I could, especially in regard to standing up to your inner bully. In the process, my goal—and my joy—was to hopefully get you to recognize and appreciate the strengths and personal gifts you have within you, strengths and gifts you have come to see your inner bully never wanted you to see—much less welcome you having them.

So for your sake, I say: keep up the good work, and thank *you.* I wish you all the best in your journey in the years ahead!

Introduction

ONE OF MY ALL-TIME FAVORITE MOVIES is Woody Allen's *Play It Again, Sam*. In this classic tale of a determined but socially klutzy protagonist named Allan Felix, Felix manages to stumble over and over in his futile efforts to fulfill his dream of finding true love and happiness after his wife shatteringly divorces him. It could be saying ridiculous things or doing bumbling things— like while being in his apartment with a date, trying to suavely and seductively pull a record album from its cover (showing my age here), only to have the record fly across the room. Whether saying the wrong thing or doing the wrong thing, Felix keeps being his own worst enemy and sabotaging his efforts.

Eventually Felix decides that what he needs is a romantic coach. Especially, he decides, he needs a coach who is a man who can charm women with his air of manly, suave self-confidence. The imaginary, alter-ego coach Felix chooses to fill this role is his screen idol from the iconic movie *Casablanca*, Humphrey Bogart. In one hilarious scene after another, his coach invisibly to everyone else coaxes and cajoles Felix into discovering his own "inner Bogie," if you will. Eventually Felix recognizes that he doesn't need a coach anymore—he's never going to be Bogie, but he will always be Allan Felix. A man who admittedly may be more than a little self-absorbed, but who nonetheless amongst other things is interesting, funny, intelligent, and certainly romantic. Those appealing qualities were just what Felix needed to remind himself in order to have chance to stop being his own worst enemy in love and romance.

So when's the last time you declared that *you* are your own worst enemy? Or that you too often beat up on yourself? Or the last time someone told you that's how *they* see you? Maybe not in those exact words, but close enough to them.

If you are starting now to read this book, then I'm figuring the chances are it was pretty recently. And certainly not for the first time, I would imagine, nor likely will it be the last.

Speaking of this book, for some time now I had wanted to write something for all of the people of the world who see themselves as all too often being their own worst enemy. People who in the process, end up sabotaging themselves in more ways than one. Maybe it's been on the job, or in school, or with romantic partners, or in any other important relationships in your life. Or maybe it's been (gulp) all of the above? In the process feeling at times like you are pretty much a version of Allan Felix yourself.

But that's not to say you can't have some very appealing qualities too. In fact, I'm going to *assume* you do. I'll even venture to guess that enough people in your life see you as definitely having appealing qualities, for example, being caring, compassionate, intelligent, hardworking, outgoing, or fun-loving. I only hope you agree that at least some of those adjectives do apply to you—and maybe a few other positive ones too? You may also be clear there are things you are accomplishing in your life that truly matter to you—again, for example, on the job front, the school front, the parenting front, or the relationship front.

Unfortunately, in spite of the good things about you and any of your accomplishments, you can still manage to beat up on yourself and be your own worst enemy anyway—in the process, making self-sabotage feel sometimes like it's virually your middle name!

That said, I must confess that the description of tending to be a self-sabotaging type of person applied to me as well, as in "been there, done that." In all honesty, that was the case for more years than I care to admit to myself—much less to anyone reading this book. Fortunately for me, though, I self-sabotage nowhere as much now as in the past.

That confession now on the table, I want whoever is reading this to know that I am not writing this book only as Dr. Sidney Cohen the psychologist. In truth, this book is being written by a "co-author" who happens to be named Sidney Cohen the person.

Here's the scoop in a nutshell about this "co-author." Since the time I was a little tot, I had a knack for—you might say—throwing *myself* under the bus. For example, I had a tendency to bully—and in the process alienate myself from—other kids on sports teams I played for by being (as a teammate once jumped down my throat and called me) a "little Napoleon." Then during many of my "guy" years in my 20's and 30's (see humor writer Dave Barry's wonderfully funny book *Complete Guide To Guys*) I often enough got accused by women who came into my life of "jumping the gun," that is, trying to prematurely become intimate, including with women with whom I wanted to have a deeper relationship. This typically led them at that point to—what a surprise—giving me the old heave-ho right out of their lives!

Eventually though, I did manage to move forward into a full-fledged, responsible adult life. Along that path, though, there were a few instances of self-sabotage that when I think about them are embarrassing enough to keep hidden in "the vault," as they say. But there's one self-sabotaging event in my past that stands out above all the others, which I am now going to share with you.

In a nutshell, a good number of moons ago when I was in my mid-forties, I had a special woman in my life named Nancy. Nancy was a woman who made it clear to me through words and actions that she loved me very much and wanted us to share a future together. She was a woman with whom I shared a great deal in common, and whom I saw as the essence of a "good soul," with totally right values. A woman who I have come to see in retrospect arguably was more right for me than any other woman who has ever been a partner of mine. And let me assure you that to this day, my eyes can still become a bit teary when I think that—simply because I feel certain that that statement is the truth, whole truth, and nothing but the truth!

Yet in the end, Nancy was the person who ultimately ended our relationship after two and a half years together. Why? Because at that point I still was unwilling to commit to a future together, even after all that time. And why was that the case, you have every reason to ask? Because I was a darn big fool, that's why! Specifically, what I managed to do was to come up with some reasons that—I'll call it "something inside me"—I believed were "valid" reasons to not build a future with Nancy. For instance, she wasn't very educated, she wasn't very sexy, she wasn't very assertive, and—wait till you hear this one—she loved me too much for my comfort level. In retrospect though, truth be told, Nancy was all of the following: a very intelligent woman, an attractive woman inside and out, a woman who asserted herself when *she* felt was the right time to assert herself (and not when *I* felt was the right time), and—best of all, but now very sadly for me when I look back—a woman who genuinely loved me for me, which of course was just the right amount!

Yes, I managed to move on from Nancy because, well, I had to if I still wanted to be in a committed long-term relationship again, which I knew I did. But like I said, something inside me really messed with my mind, not to mention my judgment and decision making, and to a degree that you could say in the end made "it" to be the clear-cut winner and me the clear-cut loser—big time.

Let me tell you what I mean by the phrase "something inside me." It's a "something" that steered me down the path of self-sabotage of my relationship with Nancy; the same something that had steered me down other paths of self-sabotage over the years; the same something that I control much better overall than I used to. But I am well aware of the same something still lurking there inside me, neither gone nor forgotten. And I know that that will be the case for as long for I am alive—not just inside me, though, but to varying degrees anway, inside of all of us..

The name to be used in this book for that something is the "inner bully."

Putting this altogether, and with double meaning fully intended, I declare that when it comes to acts of self-sabotage, believe you me, I wrote the book on the inner bully!

Let me tell you three more things about the notion of an inner bully. First, in my previous book, this notion was applied to self-sabotaging specifically on the weight-loss front (*Inner Blocks to Losing Weight: Why You Lose the Battle More Than the Weight*). In this present go-around though, I go for broke, meaning that in this book the inner bully notion gets expanded to many other life contexts besides weight loss, in which self-sabotage can unfortunately reign supreme.

Second, there are other names that have been used elsewhere as basically synonymous with the term inner "bully." For example, you've got inner "critic" (*Embracing Your Inner Critic*; Hal and Sidra Stone; 1993), inner "judge" (*Power of the Inner Judge*;

Leon Wormser; 2000), and inner "tyrant" (*Taming Your Inner Tyrant*; Patty DeLlosa; 2011). The reason I prefer inner "bully" is that years ago when I began incorporating the concept centrally into my practice, a nonscientific, informal survey I conducted made it the clear winner over those other terms. Keep in mind though as you proceed from here that I do not have a stake in your having to use the term "bully." In fact, under the proverbial "a rose is a rose" heading, please feel free if you'd prefer to replace the term with any of the other three terms covered above. Even feel free to create your *own* term (as some of my patients have chosen to do), for example, "the darkness," "Le Saboteur," "bad _____ (fill in the blank with a name)," and "the beast." What counts more than anything is that we stay on the same page in understanding the concept of an inner bully. That's especially the case in terms of finding the concept to be relevant and useful to you, and applying it in any situation where you do not want to sabotage yourself (again).

Finally, as you can see from the titles of the books just cited, the emphasis on dealing with your inner bully (or its equivalent) has been on learning to, for example, "tame" it, "embrace" it, or recognize its "power." From my perspective though, if I choose to go with the term "bully," then I'm assuming that if we're supposed to learn to stand up to *real-life* bullies—and not so much try to tame or embrace them, because that is rarely doable—then that's the better way to frame it for dealing with our inner one. Nor do I recommend framing it as trying to "beat" it, "eliminate" it, or "ignore" it—simply because none of that is do-able either. Instead, if your goal is to learn how to stand up to bullies—both the inner *and* real-life versions—it is more realistic and productive if you focus on words like "challenging" or "managing" or "asserting yourself with" them. In the end what matters more than anything is that you make sure to practice this standing-up process as consistently as possible. That's potentially your best chance to help yourself gain both the courage and the confidence to cut down on self-sabotage—hopefully more consistently than you ever have.

Before moving on to the nitty-gritty of self-sabotage and the inner bully, I want to underscore that there are quite a few excellent books already in the marketplace devoted to self-sabotage. Among the best in my view are *The Self-Sabotage Cycle: Why We Repeat Behaviors That Create Hardship and Ruin Relationships* by Stanley Rosner and Patricia Hermes (Prager Press; 2006); *What Stops You? Overcoming Self-Sabotage, Personal and Professional* by Darlene Braden (Booksurge; 2006); and "What's Your Sabotage?" by Alyce Cornyn-Selby (Beynch Press: 1990). What makes this book different from these others is its emphasis on all of the following: the concept of the inner bully, a detailed description of the psychological underpinnings of self-sabotage, and the important connection between the self-sabotaging inner bully and real bullies. Also, many of the numerous self-help strategies presented in the final two chapters of this book differ from many of the ones covered elsewhere—especially strategies like personal penance, permission work, and the use of a powerful tool for building self-respect called Self-Credit Time. In addition, and fitting with an emphasis in many places these days on spirituality, some thoughts are offered on how to tap into personal spiritual pursuits as part of the process for cutting down on self-sabotage and standing up to the inner bully.

The book is organized into two parts. Part 1 addresses the essence of what self-sabotage and the inner-bully notion/metaphor are all about. The focus then turns to the primary psychological "fuel" for the inner bully: *agitation*, defined mainly as emotional and physical "churning" inside. Next comes a chapter on one of the main psychological/circumstantial trigger and perpetuator for this core agitation: *betrayal*. This is followed by a chapter zeroing in on one of the inner bully's favorite tricks to get you to sabotage yourself, labeled "addiction to self-rebellion." The last chapter of Part 1 underscores the connection between the inner bully and its "partners in crime" steering you to self-sabotage: "outer" or *real* bullies.

Then in the three chapters of Part 2, the focus shifts to the positive side of things, that is, tools and strategies for practicing standing up to your inner bully. With the goal here being to help you cut down on your self-sabotaging ways, while in the process building up a solid core of self-esteem and self-respect. The first of the three chapters in Part 2 highlights individual self-help tools for putting your inner bully in its place. The second chapter is all about relationships and what you can do to keep your inner bully from messing them up (over and over maybe?). Finally, the third chapter is devoted to tools for cutting down on self-sabotage in the workplace. All are in one way or another geared toward strengthening your own inner Bogie/Bogette!

A little postscript if I may on the breakup of this book into two parts. In many self-help books, theory and self-help strategies tend to be presented in the same chapter. I chose not to do that here because I wanted to get all of the theory out there on the table first so that by the time you get to the three self-help chapters you will have all the input you need to really focus on self-help. Or to put that a bit differently, I opted to go the route of the "what the problems are" part first and the "what to do about them" part second. Please feel free though to jump ahead a bit at any point in Part 1—if you are inclined toward a "sneak preview" of sorts—and check out some of the self-help strategies in Part 2, before you jump right back to where you left off in Part 1.

With the outline of what's ahead covered, and without further ado, I take you to Chapter 1.

PART ONE

Chapter 1

Self-Sabotage—An Introduction

ALL TOO OFTEN, PEOPLE ARE THWARTED from reaching their most important life goals. This unfortunate reality can result not just from stressful outside forces or situational factors, but also from an inner voice that can slowly ebb at one's progress at best, or crush it in a moment like a tsunami at worst. It is precisely this self-sabotage that has led many to agree that they are their own worst enemy. Self-sabotage unfortunately is a common occurrence, and can affect your self-esteem and ability to succeed. On a note of optimism though, which I want make sure to offer you here, there are ways to get control over your self-sabotaging thoughts and behaviors. In the process, you will increase the odds of reaching your life goals, be it on the job front, the school front, the relationship front, or any front important to you. That's what this book is all about.

Following are some case examples to get a better idea of how self-sabotage affects can affect your ability to complete the goals you may set for yourself.

Sara

Sara is one of the many roller-coaster riders on the weight-loss front. Needing to lose approximately twenty pounds, Sara typically builds up momentum in the first few months by religiously adhering to a structured diet of choice. She also makes sure to exercise at least three days per week. But when she gets about halfway to her goal Sara typically gets off track by a combination of overeating, making unhealthy food choices, and not exercising. At this point, Sara ends up in the throes of self-sabotaging negative momentum, which in turn leads her right back where she started at her original weight, defined by Sara as one word only: "fat."

Marv

Marv is in a job he loves as a middle-level manager in a computer software company. After working at the company for five years, his overall professional goal is to be promoted to an upper-level management position. However, Marv's immediate boss is someone Marv thoroughly dislikes, especially given his overcritical and undercrediting style of management. Yet rather than make a concerted effort to tolerate his boss, much less bite the bullet and gratiate himself to him, what does Marv do? For months now, he has gone ahead and demonstrated just how disgruntled an employee he has become, which has translated into patterns of job-sabotaging behaviors such as chronic lateness, missing deadlines, taking a lot of nonlegitimate sick days, and generally fluctuating between being argumentative and self-isolating. As a result, Marv's boss called him on the carpet recently, which seemed to be inevitable. His boss made it clear that if these behaviors continued, not only would Marv never be promoted, his job itself would likely be in jeopardy.

Jessica

Jessica was determined to buy her own home after years of renting with no equity gained. Jessica knew she needed to be more financially disciplined than she had been in order to afford the house's down payment, but she was not a great candidate for saving money. In fact, she persisted in making risky investments, overspending on clothes and activities, and ringing up significant credit card debts. In the process, all Jessica ended up assuring herself was that she was going to be staying put in her rental apartment. As a result, frustration and disappointment reigned supreme for Jessica as she kept putting herself in a position of being forced to postpone her dream of home ownership.

Bert

Bert's most recent blood test results showed that he was heading straight to becoming a Type-2 diabetic. Bert's family doctor made it clear that if Bert didn't start eating healthier and exercising regularly, then he would be forced to live a much more restrictive lifestyle as a diabetic. Rather than heeding his doctor's advice, Bert remained an avid practitioner of denial. In the process, he proceeded to go on his merry way continuing to overeat on the sweets and carbs fronts, and to underexercise.

Debra

Debra confided in her friend Sue that she was "falling in love again" for the third time in the eight years since she had been divorced. In each of the two previous "love" episodes, things between Debra and her significant other had inevitably come to an abrupt halt. Sooner or later, Debra acted out by, e.g., losing her temper too often, drinking too much, or cheating on her partner. As a result of these relationship-undermining tendencies, it was just a matter of time before "Mr. Right" would decide that Debra was his "Ms. Wrong."

Ron

To his family, friends, and coworkers, Ron was the picture of a loyal family member, great friend, and esteemed colleague. Additionally, Ron was seen by almost everyone who knew him as an intelligent, funny, compassionate, and generous man who also had a sort of "pied piper" gift with adoring children. Nonetheless, if you asked Ron what his views on himself were, you would have to take all that positive evidence and throw it out the window. Why? Because according to Ron, he was just a big imposter. As Ron saw it, he wasn't very intelligent, likable, funny, giving, or anything else positive. In fact, according to Ron, because he never completed college, didn't make much money, felt very uncomfortable in most social gatherings, and never married or had kids, he was a failure in life. Therefore no matter how much affection, respect, and appreciation were thrown his way, Ron's core view of himself could be summed up in three words: "never good enough."

What do Sara, Marv, Jessica, Bert, Debra, and Ron share in common? These good people have the same self-defeating pattern of undermining themselves in important aspects of their life. They are members of a gang of sorts whose members all too often get caught in the throes of self-sabotage.

They differ from each though other mainly in regard to the primary life context in which their self-sabotaging manifests. For Sara, it's weight and body-image issues. Marv sabotages his career. Jessica struggles in the financial realm. Bert loses the battle for good health, and Debra undermines her romantic relationships. As for Ron, his conviction that he is nothing but a failure in life, no matter how much circumstantial evidence to the contrary, cuts across many fronts.

After reviewing these examples, do you see a pattern of self-sabotage in any areas of your own life? Are you basically a clone of Sara, Marv, Jessica, Bert, Debra, or Ron? Maybe some combination of them? Even if you only sabotage yourself on a limited number of fronts, you may already have paid a price in terms of your core self-worth.

Self-esteem. Self-respect. Self-confidence. Self-assurance. Self-worth. We hear a lot of these terms in one place or another, but what do they really mean? In this book, Self-worth (SW) is defined in the form of an equation: SW = SE (self-esteem) + SR (self-respect).

Let's break this down further. There are two possible definitions of SE. One can be considered the traditional definition of SE while the other would be the preferred definition of SE.

Traditional Versus Preferred Definition of Self-Esteem

From my perspective, how satisfied you are with your physical appearance can play a strong role in your self-esteem. I think it's safe to say that physical appearance counts even more for women than for men. Many women can attest to the times when an out-of-place hair, a newly discovered wrinkle, or a perceived extra jiggle can cause a serious drop in their self-esteem despite the fact that they might be intelligent, hardworking, and accomplished. In these times, a woman looks in the mirror and sees someone who is unappealing–even if at the same time she may recognize she has truly likable and appealing personal qualities on the "inside."

The impact that physical appearance has on a woman's self-esteem has resulted from a long process of socialization and conditioning. Advertisements, talk shows, books, and magazine articles all reinforce the misguided notion that a woman's primary worth is in her external beauty. Additionally and unfortunately, people tend to compliment women more on their appearance than any other quality they have, including truly likable and appealing qualities on the "inside."

Of course, physical appearance does matter to men. However, any physical flaws such as being overweight, going bald, or being on the small size generally do not cause men to downgrade what makes them feel good about themselves.

On a lighter note, let me tell you about one of my favorite cartoons of all time. The cartoon contains a captionless split panel. One panel depicts a well-built woman looking at herself in the mirror. Unfortunately, she sees an obese, unappealing specimen as her reflection. In the other panel, a big-bellied, noticeably nondapper guy looks at himself in the mirror and sees a "true stud." Does that say it all about gender differences regarding the connection between physical appearance and self-esteem or what?

Since the popular traditional definition of self-esteem tends to be heavily influenced by your perception of your physical appearance, I would like to offer an alternative definition of self-esteem: the positive and likable personality traits and qualities you recognize within yourself on the inside. Examples: intelligence, passion, sense of humor, ambition, compassion, sensitivity, devotion, sensuality, generosity, and sociability. With this added definition of self-esteem, you are focusing on lasting and genuine qualities rather than just those of a superficial nature.

What are the odds that we can begin to base our self-esteem on our internal characteristics more than our usual focus on outward appearances? A proverbial "slim and none and slim left town" of a chance if you ask me. Yet I maintain that we should all try to gradually create more of a balance between the two. Within the next year, we may not be able to reach the point where our internal qualities override the external ones in determining our self-esteem. However, a realistic goal would be getting to the point where our self-esteem is equally connected to what we like about ourselves on the outside *and* the inside. For example, if you find yourself obsessing over your weight but are then able to tell yourself "I may have a few unwanted extra pounds but I'm actually really likable in many ways on the inside," that would be a significant breakthrough on the self-esteem front. Once you have reminded yourself enough times of that very positive internal self-assessment, by Jove, you've got it– got real self-esteem that is! At the end of this chapter, you will find an exercise that will assist you in learning how to focus more on those internal positive qualities.

Self-Respect

For quite some time now, it has been striking to me how many people use terms like "self-esteem," "self-confidence," and "self-assured" much more naturally than the term "self-respect." I'm not really sure why that's the case. I only know that I believe that having a solid core of self-respect counts more than anything in building a strong foundation of self-worth. That's especially the case if we define self-respect as anything you are doing in your life that gives you at least a little sense of accomplishment.

The key word here actually is "little." To gain self-respect, you don't have to have major accomplishments like completing an education, getting a great job, or being a devoted spouse and/or parent. Certainly significant accomplishments like these can go a long way to making your self-respect level high. Nevertheless, when it comes to self-respect, your "little" accomplishments count every bit as much as the major ones. These "little" achievements, the ones we all tend to downplay or take for granted as not being worthy of any kind of special acknowledgment, really do add up over time.

Here are some examples of what I am labeling "little" accomplishments. How about: effort, self-control, goals met, creativity, acts of giving and compassion, and, last but goodness knows not least, acts of courage. These are just all those things we are simply "supposed to" do in life and therefore should basically take for granted and not make any big deal about, right? Wrong. Big-time wrong!

To cut to the chase, there are two things I think we all need to keep in mind here. First, the only way to reach our biggest goals in life is by doing the little stuff, yet we all tend to take the little stuff for granted. Truth be told, we should be doing exactly the opposite for ourselves on a daily basis, that is, giving ourselves a little bit of credit for doing the little stuff. Second, it's in our control each day to do the little stuff, whereas reaching any of our big goals can take many months if not years.

What are these little accomplishments that I mentioned? First, there's *effort*. Effort is any physical or mental hard work you did that day. Then there's *self-control*, something you did that involved keeping some self-defeating act or habit of yours under control. Next is *goals met*, defined as anything you did that represented having reached some important goal you had hoped to reach by the end of that day. Then we have *creativity*, whatever you did that involved you being creative in some way, for example, artistically, domestically, or humorously. Number five on the hit parade are *acts of giving/compassion*, which are things you did that involved you giving something important to someone whether it be money, material, time, or physical assistance and/or showing compassion to someone. Last but not least—in fact, the least little of them all—are *acts of courage*. My working definition of these acts is anything you are reluctant or hesitant to do but you make yourself do it anyway because it's in your best interest to do so.

Allow me to expand on that very important definition of courage. As I think of it, except for true love (of any relationship type), very little counts more in life than the exercise of courage. For example, it's certainly an act of courage for someone with a public-speaking phobia to give a speech in front of a large group. It also can take a great deal of courage to return to school to complete a long-sought-after academic degree after being out of school for many years. Maybe your act of courage is to assert yourself with someone important to you who has a tendency to be very critical and judgmental by letting the person know loud and clear that you feel really angry or hurt over something he or she said or did to you. Perhaps your act of courage is opposite of the above, that is, asking a person important to you to forgive you.

Keep in mind that a separate category of acts of courage exists too. This is the generally more obvious category, involving confronting some type of potential physical danger or threat such as intervening in an act of observed violence or pursuing a major physical challenge like skydiving. I think it's safe to say that these are examples of the stereotypical definition of courage. Yes, for sure these can be noteworthy and respectable acts of courage. But they are for the most part isolated acts. The acts of courage that cover the little things we do each day count more for true self-respect than those quite courageous but isolated acts of physically confronting danger or challenges.

As you can imagine, these little acts of courage are virtually guaranteed over time to trigger a good deal of true pride and accomplishment inside, not the bragging or conceited type of pride. Instead, it's what I like to call the *foundational* type of pride. This is the "quiet" but self-respecting feeling you can get when you do something truly beneficial to your personal growth, which therefore makes any and every act of courage a real gift from you to you.

The main reason I break self-respect down into these six aforementioned components is because if you adopt this view, then it doesn't matter whether you make a lot of money, live in a fancy house, drive a sports car, or are physically attractive. If you work on developing these six areas in your life, you are guaranteed to feel a good deal of respect for yourself no matter what else you have or don't have going for you. At the end of this chapter, there will be an additional exercise to assist you in working toward developing in the areas of self-respect.

Approach/Avoidance Conflict and Self-Sabotage

One day during a session in my office, a patient, Joe, and I were reviewing his work on some exercises he had finished during the previous week. Joe had listed five likable personal traits: being outgoing, giving, intelligent, loyal, and affectionate. Additionally, Joe was making progress in two of the components that increase self-respect each time he reviewed his daily accomplishments.

Sounds pretty positive, right? Well, it was except for one catch. Joe stated, "Doc, I figure I must be a good person if I know I have these five really good qualities. I feel like I must be accomplishing something in my life if I keep meeting a couple of categories for self-respect, but I have to level with you. I still don't really *believe* these good things about myself. It's like something in me is saying, 'Hey, Joe, you can list all of the positives you want to list about yourself, but don't you start believing for one second that you actually *are* a likable and respectable person!' I do these exercises because I know it's a good idea for me to do them, but the truth is, they really don't benefit me much at all, Doc, in all honesty."

Tune in to a later chapter when I talk about how someone like Joe can recondition himself to believe that he is in fact allowed or has *permission* to believe as many good things about himself as there may be on both the self-esteem and self-respect fronts. For now, I will simply propose that Joe's inability to believe that he deserves to give himself credit where credit is due is a cognitive and emotional act of pure self-sabotage. Yes, Joe came up with five items on his Self-Esteem list, but he struggled to do that. In fact, he required three suggestions from his trusty friend, Marla, to add to his original list of only two items. Yes, Joe checked off a category or two each time he made progress in the components of self-Respect. However, none of that changes the fact, as Joe told me many times, that he kept feeling like anything he did that met one or more categories was all just "trivial" and "no big deal at all."

Therefore, we pretty much end up with a good news/bad news scenario here for Joe and for enough other people in the world whose core self-Worth isn't where they wish it would or could be. The good news is that Joe did his best for a while keeping his commitment to looking at his Self-Esteem list and working on improving his self-Respect. The bad news is that it gave him little if any satisfaction or consolation to do this. In fact, after a few more weeks, Joe stopped using both of these exercises entirely. In the process, self-sabotage won while Joe's self-Worth lost.

In the 1960s, psychologists John Dollard and Neal Miller carried out some thought-provoking experiments on what they labeled "approach/avoidance" conflicts. The subjects of their experiments were some hardy but harassed white laboratory rats. In these studies, a hungry rat was placed at beginning of a specially constructed wooden runway. Mr./Ms. Rat proceeded to scurry down the runway to get to the inviting feast of a food dish. About halfway there though, a strong electric shock was delivered to the poor little fella/gal. The rat immediately recoiled in pain and beat a fast retreat up the runway to literally lick his/her wounds. Inevitably, though, hunger would return, at which point the rat would do an about-face and scamper back down the runway again only to freeze when about to reach the recently discombobulating shock point. Back and forth each rat went in the runway, for however long the researchers kept the experiment going. In the process, none of the rats ever actually fulfilled their food "quest," at least not until the experimenters ended up directly feeding the rat after all.

Dollard and Miller concluded that the "volunteers" in their study developed a post-shock approach/avoidance conflict. When the hungry shocked rat was still at a distance from the food goal, it approached the goal full speed ahead, but once it was right about at the shock point, it stopped dead in its tracks and headed back to the hills, never coming close to the craved food dish down the runway.

You may ask, "What does this semi-sadistic-sounding experiment with lab rats have to do with us humans?" Let me put it this way. If we substitute a rat-related food goal for a human-related self-Worth goal, and electric shock for a psychological shock, then Dollard and Miller's experiments become just as relevant to us two-legged creatures. If you were working on building up your self-Esteem, you would proceed to do what's in your control to do to gradually make that happen. For example, you may begin working on some self-Worth-building exercises, but at some point while you are "approaching" your goal, you discontinue the work needed to get there. That's when you can think of yourself as heading squarely in the "avoidance" direction, otherwise known as self-sabotage!

Addiction to Self-Sabotage

Self-sabotage can actually become a full-fledged addiction. Addiction can be seen as having two parts. The first is any behavior in control of you rather than you in control of the behavior. The second part of addiction results from the first: the behavior that controls you causes you some type of harm whether it's psychological, physical, financial, or interpersonal. In enough instances, it can be all of the above.

This definition of addiction fits the usual types of addictions out there. More importantly, though, the definition applies to *any* pattern or behavior that you have exhibited over the years that falls under the heading of self-sabotage, not just the more commonly known addictions. The key word here is *pattern*. It is a pattern of doing things to undermine your romantic relationships, your job, and/or your financial security. Of course dependence on drugs or alcohol, compulsive gambling, compulsive overeating and other types of substance addictions all have specific patterns themselves, and they all are examples of self-sabotage addiction.

Similarly, as when dealing with these commonly known addictions, broad-scoped addiction to self-sabotage takes a great deal of sustained effort to conquer. Just remember: no one wants, needs, or enjoys sabotaging himself/herself, yet people continue to engage in the same behaviors over and over again. Clearly, if you keep sabotaging yourself despite negative consequences, then you have a lot of work ahead of you to get this addiction under control once and for all.

The "Culprit"

Who is the "culprit" behind your self-sabotaging? He/she/it can be thought of as a negative "force" in your subconscious, a force that acts as though it has little if any conscience, has nothing better to do than to keep trying to steer you toward undermining yourself in some truly aggravating way. On a Star Trekkie note, may this force *not* be with you, except that unfortunately we all have no choice in the matter. The name I have given to this force is the "inner bully." Look at it this way. If a real-life person kept harassing you and in the process made you feel pretty lousy about yourself, wouldn't you feel that this person is a bully? What I'm doing here then is creating a metaphor for the inner equivalent of a real bully. Tricks your inner bully uses against you and how to stand up to it will be presented later in this book.

As a little addendum here, feel free to exchange the term inner bully with the term "ego." For some of you, that may be the term you already use in regards to the part of you inside that you think of as the source of your self-sabotaging ways.

In summary, the main points of this chapter are the following:

1. Self-sabotage can occur in a wide variety of significant life contexts from schooling to one's job or career, or to personal relationships.

2. Self-Worth represents the combination of self-Esteem and self-Respect.

3. Self-sabotage mainly reflects undermining of that self-Worth.

4. The inner driving force behind self-sabotage is the negative part of the subconscious previously labeled as "the inner bully."

I'd like to offer one postscript though before having you do some exercises related to self-Esteem and self-Respect. I happen to be a big fan of acronyms, and here's one of my favorites in my work: PACF. This stands for "push," "action," "courage," and "fulfillment." Let me translate this for you in motivational and behavioral terms. Starting with *push*, the idea here is to push—which really means *force*—yourself to do things you have been avoiding doing, quite possibly for quite a while now. For example, you push and force yourself to begin a home remodeling project, or pursue returning to school, or make a major relationship change.

Once you have pushed yourself hard to get yourself going, the pushing must translate into taking some kind of constructive *action*. Suppose, for example, you have for a long time now wanted to go back to school. In the process, you have come up with explanations for not doing that, some of which may be legitimate reasons (for example, expense), while some of them may well be excuses more than explanations (for example, you don't have the intelligence or drive to do so, much less to do well).

But now let's suppose there is no longer an overriding expense issue preventing you from going back to school, be it for a college degree, an associate's degree, or some type of specialized training. The issue at that point is likely to boil down to one thing: anxiety-based *avoidance*. If you are being totally honest with yourself and you face the fact that pure unadulterated avoidance is what it boils down to, then you must push yourself to take action. Basically, you give yourself no choice, that is, you *must* now go ahead and send out applications to the school or program of your preference. That's taking action, right?

Once you put the long-delayed, appropriate plan into action, you have brought *courage* into the picture. Courage in my view does not precede action as much as it develops once you have *taken* action. Sticking with the school example, it didn't take courage to get you to finally take action to go back to school as much as it took, again, pushing yourself to take the action. Then once you take the step, courage sets in if you then proceed to carry the action through to the finish!

And if all goes well, this will lead to the final link in this productive/constructive chain of events: *fulfillment*. I am defining fulfillment here as eventually reaching your specific goal, which began with pushing yourself to take action in the first place, followed by getting the courage to stick with it until the goal is reached. It doesn't matter whether the fulfillment comes from reaching goals like getting a degree, getting a better job, completing a major project around the house, or making the quality of some important relationships in your life better. All that matters is that you proceed to the end of the PACF chain.

And if you manage to do all that, then consider it nothing short of a major victory over your inner bully. How can it not be, if in the end what that fulfillment of whatever type boils down to is a big gain in your self-Respect? This in turn, rest assured, will annoy the inner bully to no end!

Now to the exercises.

Exercise #1: "My Self-Esteem List"

Make a list of one- or two-word adjectives of all the positive personality traits you recognize in yourself. Don't worry if you are only able to come up with three or four traits initially. The quality of the traits you list counts much more than quantity. As long as they are truly positive traits, that is good enough for now, and you may end up adding a lot more to the list over time. If there are some traits you are considering writing down but you are thinking, "Well, I'm only like that sometimes but not all the time," put them on the list if you feel you have those qualities more often than not. Take your time completing your list. It's only to your benefit that you put your heart and soul into it.

Once you have completed listing your positive internal traits, give yourself the option of adding anything that you like about your physical appearance to the list. Here's the catch, though. If you choose to put anything down on paper about your appearance, you must first draw a line under the last item on your original list. Anything positive you list about your physical appearance will be written below that line. In this way, you are making an important symbolic statement literally on paper: "What I like about myself on the inside (above the line) counts more than what I like about myself on the outside (below the line)."

Once you have completed this step, give yourself the option of showing it to someone you trust. The purpose in doing this is to give that person the opportunity to recommend any additions to your list. Only positive traits here can be recommended, never any negative. For each item the chosen person indicates, you get "veto power." In other words, if you agree with the traits/qualities the person proposes, then thank him/her and add the trait to your list. If there are any suggestions for your list that you cannot recognize in yourself, you can still thank the person but don't put the suggestions on your list.

Last but not least, whenever you feel you've gone as far with your list as you can, transcribe it onto a small sheet of paper. Then make sure to look at that Self-Esteem list at least once a day. The more times a day you look, the merrier. Looking at your list is not going to leave you feeling anything earthshaking or greatly uplifting, but it can leave you with a nice boost to your spirits and ultimately to your true self-esteem. This is basically the opposite of self-sabotage, don't you think?

Exercise #2: "Self-Credit Time"

This exercise involves the use of a structured tool to recondition yourself to focus more on your daily "little" accomplishments and less on your long-term major successes as the basis of giving yourself some credit where credit is due. Before bedtime, give yourself some time to reflect on anything you did that day that fits into any of the six categories listed above that help increase self-respect, that is, effort, self-control, creativity, goals met, acts of giving/compassion, and courage. You only have to acknowledge one category you met, but if you feel you met more than one that day—for example, you worked very hard at the office (effort), kept to your diet (self-control), and went out of your way to help a neighbor (act of giving and compassion)—then by all means give yourself credit in multiple categories. Also, save a written log of this. Keep each entry as brief as possible so you don't end up feeling it's a chore to complete this exercise. Last but not least, feel free to do this exercise proactively and not just retroactively. Once or twice per week, set a goal for yourself that you will do something to meet a particular category, especially courage, within the next forty-eight hours. Assuming you met the goal, go ahead and make darn sure you log the fact that you made this accomplishment.

Chapter 2

Your Self-Sabotaging Inner Bully

"You're really stupid! You're lazy! You're ugly! You'll never amount to anything! I'm very disappointed in you! I wish you were never born!"

Have you ever been on the receiving end of any of these types of truly nasty declarations, especially from either one or both of your parents/guardians, another relative, a friend, a teacher, or a coach? Statements like these could be considered communicational "sucker punches" delivered squarely into the receiver's emotional gut, the kind of "punches" that are the verbal equivalent of an actual physical punch to the actual gut. These types of verbal punches can be labeled "bullying" and can cut deeply into your emotional core.

As we have seen especially in the past decade, educators, researchers, politicians, and certainly parents have taken episodes of verbal tormenting and elevated—or should I say lowered—them to the same condemnable level as physical abuse. In fact, in my professional experience, being on the receiving end of ongoing verbal abuse/bullying typically can create deeper and more lasting psychological scars than physical bullying. Sure, the latter may leave physical scars; but it's the verbal form than can penetrate deeper, not just into your body but deep down into your heart and soul.

How do we define a true bully? There are lots of definitions out there, but here's the one I use in my work. A bully is a person who engages in a pattern of harm-intending, victimizing, verbal, and/or physical behavior that in the process reflects four unseemly characteristics or traits on the bully's part: (1) acts like he/she has no conscience; (2) can be relentless; (3) hits you when you're down; and (4) gets used to you not fighting back. It does not matter one bit whether the bully is a stereotypical schoolyard Neanderthal, a gang member, a parent, a relative, a teacher, a boss, or a clergyman. Bullies are bullies, and that's the name of that tune as they say.

If someone in your life keeps telling you that you are stupid, ugly, or worthless, chances are you will end up in some form hearing those abusive words echoing in your conscious mind. At those moments, no one at all may be physically present filling the role of being a bully toward you. The fact that no one is physically present does not matter though, because when these harshly judgmental words echo in your mind, it is as though you are in the throes of bullying *yourself*.

Please be clear: I am not implying that people purposely and intentionally bully themselves into psychological submission. This is absolutely not the case. From my perspective, there ultimately is no such thing as self-bullying; that would boil down to verbal/mental "masochism." As you may know, masochism refers to a physical form of sexual behavior intended to provide the masochist with pleasure through the infliction of pain. What can sound like self-bullying is nonsexual of course. But like masochism, it is intended to cause pain. After all, hearing abusive, self-directed words like "stupid," "lazy," or "unlovable" running through your mind can create a whole lot of pain, emotionally and mentally. This tendency can therefore make you look and sound like one heck of a masochist, but rest assured that's not at all the case.

The Conscious Mind Versus the Subconscious Mind

As has been said since time immemorial, the brain is a fascinating and remarkable creation. Along those lines, neuroscience has taken the whole subject of anatomy, physiology, and functioning of the brain to levels reflective of—pardon the pun—brilliant brains at work. All kinds of evidence are increasingly being accumulated to establish objective truths about the brain. Yet in many ways the brain remains a mystery.

From my perspective though, our *mind* is every bit as big a mystery as the brain itself. When I say *mind*, I'm referring to the part of our brain that is not a tangible, structural part of our brain at all. Yet it certainly can be thought of as having a—pardon another pun—mind of its own in there for sure!.

Complicating matters of the mind even more is that there are assumed to be two separate but related parts of the mind:

the conscious and the subconscious. The conscious mind is the part containing all thoughts, memories, emotions, and fantasies we can be aware of at any given moment. For example, when you are thinking about what you have to do at work tomorrow, remembering your recent vacation, feeling frustrated, or fantasizing about an exciting sexual encounter, your conscious mind's "button" is being pressed "on."

Now suppose you are not consciously aware of any of these thoughts, memories, feelings, or fantasies. Just because you are not consciously aware of them doesn't mean they don't exist somewhere inside your mind. In fact, any and all of the thoughts, memories, emotions, and fantasies you have *ever* had are all stored in some nonconscious place in your mind. This place is understood to be the *sub*conscious.

One of my former patients likened the subconscious to an internal personal computer. Just like a real computer, the subconscious has millions of pieces of information stored up inside it, but in order to access that information in a real computer, you first have to turn the computer on, type in some key words, and then voilà—the information is likely to appear.

When it comes to our subconscious "computer" however, there are two important differences from the real ones. First, when you try to consciously access certain pieces of information in your subconscious computer, you are far from guaranteed you will actually be able to access it. For example, if you want to remember where you left your keys this morning, get clear as to what strong emotion is being buried inside you at the moment, or come up with an idea for the next chapter of your novel, there is no guarantee that turning on your subconscious computer will bring that information up.

Second, sometimes, even when you turn on your subconscious computer, it manages to bring up information stored in there anywhere. After all, how else to explain how you may suddenly become aware of a spontaneous recollection of funny lines from a movie, a sudden rush of anxiety for no apparent reason, or a fantasy of being invited onto Oprah Winfrey's show to discuss your newly published book? (Guess whose fantasy that one is?)

In other words, you might say, our subconscious computer has a mind of its own!

The Subconscious "Inner Echo"

It's time to now focus on a specific form of information stored up in our subconscious computer starting very early on in our lives. This critical information involves communications we received growing up, especially from our parents but possibly significant others too. These communications were, like all communications from one human being to another, verbal in some instances and nonverbal in others.

Some of those communications were basically positive while others were clearly negative. Positive communications include verbal expressions of love, appreciation, and respect as well as nonverbal expressions such as hugs, kisses, smiles, and a warm tone of voice. Negative communications are the polar opposite, for example, expressions of resentment, dislike, and disrespect and nonverbal communication including frowns, critical tone of voice, lack of eye contact, and scarcity of physical or verbal affection.

What happens to this ongoing accumulation of communications presented to anyone by parents and significant others? They don't just store up inside your subconscious computer. In fact, they pretty much take on a life of their own. Allow me to call that communicational life inside us the "inner echo."

Here's how it works. Again, assume your subconscious computer's "hard drive" takes in and then stores all the communications—positive and negative alike—directed at you from when you were a child right up to the present. With efficiency galore, you might say, your subconscious computer determines which communications are most memorable, as well as essentially the best summarized. Whether they are either positive or negative communications, your subconscious computer narrows the field down to a few basic summaries. On the positive front, these communications are likely to be along the lines of "you are truly lovable," "you are very intelligent," or "you are someone I respect a great deal." In contrast, on the negative front, the messages are likely to be in the categories of "you are unlovable" or "you are pretty worthless."

Once these summary positive and negative communications are firmly in place, they become what you can think of as an "echo" inside your subconscious mind and sometimes even in your conscious mind. It is a so-called echo that reverberates inside you, sometimes in clear words and other times in the form of aggravating "static." It's an echo that when entering your conscious mind can leave you feeling really good about yourself (positive communications) or really lousy about yourself (negative communications).

"Direct Hits" Versus "Sneak Attacks"

Allow me to zero in now on the *negative* echo that can reverberate around inside your subconscious. For starters, a distinction needs to be made between two different but related sets of communications that can feed the negative echo inside us: *direct hits* and *sneak attacks*. Direct hits are negative communications that are direct verbal put-downs or belittling repeated over and over. These are, once again, harshly judgmental words, like dumb, ugly, stupid, or useless. Sneak attacks, on the other hand, compose the *non*verbal portion of your negative echo, especially nonverbal cues like a cold tone of voice, a sour or angry face, a waving or pointing finger, or a tense, rigid body posture. Sneak attacks can also include overall patterns of negative communication, such as guilt-tripping, negative comparisons to others, neglect, or outright abandonment.

The most psychologically harmful direct hits and sneak attacks are likely to come from one or both parents. Certainly, significant others may have directed these two types of communications at you at one time or another. If that in fact was the case, you can think of negative communications like these as having an "added insult to injury" element because such communications were thrown your way by your own parents.

However, there's something else important to keep in mind. The very same parent that subjected you to direct hits and/or sneak attacks very likely also loves you very much, even if it may not feel that way to you at all! In other words, chances are that both the positive *and* negative sides of the parental-emotional equation have been communicated to you over time. The problem develops when the negative echo's voice inside you remains much louder than the positive one. That's when the combination of direct hits and sneak attacks foisted upon you can leave you feeling as though you are more *un*lovable than lovable at the core.

The subject of direct hits and sneak attacks is one I speak of not just professionally but personally as well. Yes, I definitely loved my parents and vice versa. Yet truthfully I can recall all too many instances in which both of them directed some sneak attacks my way (rarely was I on the receiving end of direct hits), especially negative comparsions and neglect on the time/attention/affection fronts. Yet I can assure you that I am well aware that any parent is quite capable of genuinely loving you anyway, even while hurling direct hits and/or sneak attacks at you in different ways at different times.

Negative Inner Echo and the Inner Bully

The essential nature of your negative inner echo is to *bully* you into believing that it's telling you the truth, the whole truth, and nothing but the truth about your worth as a person. Now that's some seriously distressing bullying, wouldn't you agree? The inner bully takes the negative internal echo and runs with it. In other words, the inner echo is the "voice" of your inner bully. It is a voice not of rational reason, to say the least, but one that can make you feel pretty crummy about yourself at the core more often than not, and for no good reason at all.

The "Ventriloquist"

I encourage you to never underestimate the resourcefulness of your inner bully in its quest to create as many instances of self-sabotage for you as it can. A prime example of this is how your inner bully uses the negative internal echo to its advantage. Let's once again go under the assumption that your inner bully exists inside your subconscious from early on in your life. That gives it plenty of opportunity during your growing years to learn to mimic the right words and the tone of voice used when either direct hits or sneak attacks were directed at you from your parents or significant others.

As if that's not creative enough for your inner bully, let's now assume your inner bully has just as much opportunity over time to learn *your own* words and voice as well, especially your self-critical words and tone of voice. If we put these two learned voices together—the echo voice of your parents plus your own voice—then your inner bully becomes capable of converting your inner echo into self-recrimination. For example, suppose you sometimes hear yourself in your mind making statements like "God, you really are stupid!" or "You know, you really are fat and ugly!" Hearing self-disparaging statements like these in your mind represent the inner bully's mimicry of previous direct hits and sneak attacks.

To put all of this a bit differently, what your inner bully learns to do over time can be thought of as a form of internal *ventriloquism*. After all, isn't any good ventriloquist able to speak in another voice and in other words besides his/her own? Additionally, what is the "vessel" through which a ventriloquist speaks? It's called a dummy—which for all intent and purpose is what your "master ventriloquist" your inner bully is able to make *you* feel like inside whenever you become very self-critical!

I recognize that it may sound like I'm really stretching the definition of ventriloquism here. But I hope it makes sense to you as a way to understand and conceptualize how your inner bully can use this unique form of ventriloquism to keep you on the path of low self-Worth and too many instances of self-sabotaging acts.

In fact, by using this perspective, you begin to have a fighting chance to stop being fooled as often as you may have been by your inner bully. This will most certainly take consciously reminding yourself over and over that your self-critical/self-condemning thoughts are not thoughts that *you* are putting into your mind. Instead, the perspective you need to adopt is that it's your "inner ventriloquist," the inner bully, who is responsible for doing that. By frequently reminding yourself of this, you will eventually become more consistent in challenging all of those negative thoughts you are hearing in your head. It's just your inner bully, "the ventriloquist," messing with your mind again! Of course, this kind of consciousness-raising will not work all the time by any stretch. However, if even sometimes it helps you nip some of your negative thinking in the bud, that's a victory for you and a defeat for your inner bully.

The "Inner Courtroom"

Here's another analogy I use regarding the inner bully. Think of there being a courtroom inside your subconscious. Presiding over this courtroom is the "(Dis-) Honorable Judge Inner Bully." The courtroom also has a prosecuting attorney and a defendant. Assume that this is a bench trial and there is no jury.

The way the courtroom works is this. The prosecuting attorney presents the crime for which the defendant is charged. As you may have figured out by now, the defendant is *you*. The crime that you are being charged with represents anything your inner bully has been criticizing you for. For example, you forgot your significant other's birthday. Perhaps you didn't complete the assignment given to you by your boss or client. Maybe you are a student who expects a grade of A in every class but you end up getting a C. Maybe you consider yourself a religious person but often find yourself not going to church as well as lying a lot. I assume you get the picture of what these "charges" against you can look like.

The bottom line is that once the prosecuting attorney informs "Judge Inner Bully" about these charges against you, the judge immediately raps its gavel and declares you guilty as charged. That's where it ends. You do not even have a defense attorney to gather witnesses of your own or cross-examine those of the prosecutor. Then to top it off, your "sentence" is likely to be a continuation of any guilt and agitation you already may be experiencing, which in turn can manifest clinically as depression and/or anxiety.

As noted previously, people with low core self-Worth tend to go around making statements like "I beat up on myself a lot" and "I'm my own worst enemy." In light of both the "ventriloquist" perspective and the "inner courtroom" perspective, from this moment on, practice reminding yourself that it's your *inner bully* that beats up on you and is your own worst enemy, not you!

The Bully's "Curse Words"

From my perspective, there is a way to characterize the underlying message created by direct hits and sneak attacks. This message, which over time becomes a core belief, can be thought of as your inner bully's two favorite "curse words." One revolves around what you do or do not *deserve*. I abbreviate that one as: the "D-word." The other focuses on self-defined *failure*, abbreviated as the "F-word."

Allow me to translate your inner bully's core message with regard to the D-word. The message always has a negative connotation. The *don't* deserve piece you can think of as basically boiling down to "You don't deserve to be happy and get what you want in your life!" The *deserve* on the other hand piece basically is

"You deserve to be punished or pay some price in some way each time you screw up something important!" Quite the unnerving double whammy from your inner bully, don't you think?

According to your inner bully, the price you will pay for your screwup, whether it's on the job, financially, or in a relationship, is to suffer some temporary blow to your self-Worth, at the very least. The other basic message here from your "hit man," the inner bully, is "Yes, you can go ahead and proceed through life trying to be happy and get what you want in important contexts of your life. However, as for you actually *becoming* happy and getting what you want in your life...well, the answer to whether you truly deserve that happiness basically is 'No way, José!'" That inner bully–instilled, self-sabotaging belief virtually guarantees that while you may have times in your life when you are feeling good about yourself, the chances nonetheless are that the good feelings you are having will be short-lived and outweighed by your ongoing not-very-good feelings.

What your inner bully does not want you to recognize is that you have the right to feel you deserve to get what you want in your life and be happy when you're clear you have *earned* it. For example, if you want a job promotion, you certainly will have a better chance of deserving that promotion if you have worked hard on job assignments and put in long hours including overtime to earn that promotion. Similarly, if you want to have a special romantic relationship and feel happy in it, in order for you to believe you deserve that special relationship, you and your significant other will have to work hard to make that relationship the best it can be. In this context of making a successful relationship, the hard work mainly involves what you can think of as the critical three *C*'s: communication, compromise, and courage. Do that ongoing work and you and your partner can say, "Hey, we've earned how solid we are together because we work at it!"

The inner bully's other favorite curse word is the "F-word" *failure*. Your inner bully's ultimate victory over you comes when it gets you to judge yourself in some way, much less in every way, as a "failure." For example, you may judge yourself in positive terms about how you do on your job, in the role of parent, or in your ability to complete domestic tasks. The bottom line here is that even if it's just one area of your life in which you feel like a failure, that can be bad enough for you on the self-Worth front because your inner bully can convince you deep down that your "failure(s)" definitely outweigh your successes.

Most people who come into my office feel like they have failed in some way, shape, or form in their lives. However, the chances are strong that this is in the person's own eyes only and no one else's. This harsh self-judgment of being a "failure" is, as I often bluntly call it, pure "bull" from your bully!

What certainly is not "bull" at all though is the harmful and lasting negative psychological effect that a self-judgment as a failure can have on you. Most harmful—and therefore creating the most self-sabotage—is what self-judgment as a failure can do to your core self-Worth. Because of that temporary, if not indefinite, undercutting of your self-Worth, this "f-word" is a bigger curse word than you-know-which f-word! After all, the latter may sting you on the surface. But when it comes to the failure f-word, you aren't just being stung. Instead, you are being cut open to the emotional core in your heart and soul, because what the failure f-word can do to you in terms of the inner bully–induced emotional pain it creates for you is to leave you with a hefty dose of guilt, if not outright shame. Those doses are mainly why I say that the failure-word is a bigger curse word psychologically than the standard f-word.

At moments like these, I am reminded of a wise old friend and mentor of mine from many moons ago. This humble but exceptionally intuitive and compassionate man by the name of Sy Green once told me there are only two types of failure in life. The first one is making no concerted effort at all to reach a goal you claim is important for you to reach. The second is the inherent failure as a so-called human being of willfully, callously, and aggressively hurting another human being or animal typically out of spite and with no conscience or remorse. In these two contexts of using the word failure, I wholeheartedly agree with my old friend Sy's notion of there being a legitimate and appropriate judgment of a person as specifically fail*ing* in the first case but being a full-blown fail*ure* in the second case. In these two contexts, the use of the word failure is not an unwarranted use of this curse word. On the contrary, it is totally warranted. In every other context, though, it is entirely *un*warranted—except of course in the twisted and twisting opinion of your inner bully.

There you have it—the inner mastermind of messing with your mind, of making sure you come up with one way or another to sabotage yourself. Unlike the immortal Wizard of Oz, who turned out to just be a quiet little man with a loud and menacing facade, the inner bully is a "wizard" who genuinely *is* loud and menacing!

As I stated in the introduction to this book, I feel it's important for anyone reading this book to know that your author certainly has had his own share of inner bullying to contend with over the course of his life. Truth be told, I spent a good part of my growing years, right up into middle-age adult life, really running up against my own inner bully's all-too-frequent imposition on me of the "d-word" and the "f-word." In the process, I was left feeling that my professional self-Worth couldn't have been much higher, yet on the other hand, my personal self-Worth was significantly lower. In other words, my inner bully has won a whole lot more victories over me on the personal front compared to my professional life.

Thankfully though, that has changed enough over the years so I can safely say I am now the victor over my inner bully more than it is victorious over me, a fact for which I am genuinely grateful. But hear me loud and clear here when I say to you: my inner bully can still at times kick my butt with the best (and therefore worst) of them!

It is also important to keep in mind the unfortunate but unavoidable reality that the inner bully is never going to go away. In fact, the goal should never be to try to get rid of or "knock off" much less "knock *out*" your inner bully. That's not going to happen. Think of the sabotaging workings of the inner bully are like to the amusement park game where the moles keep popping up, and no matter how many times you whack them on their heads to disappear, others seem to keep reappearing. Instead of trying to whack or kill your *it*, it is more realistic to make your goal be *standing up* to your inner bully. Do your best at that no matter how much your inner bully may taunt you into submission to its self-sabotaging tricks of its trade.

Look at it this way. If your inner bully is actually pretty tame, then the chances are you will not sabotage yourself with any consistency or in any important areas of your life. Even when you do sabotage yourself in some way, the odds are you will pick yourself up off the floor pretty quickly, in a healthy, nonbullying way. That in turn can allow you to chalk it up to a personal-growth learning experience. From my perspective though, regarding your overall mental health and life satisfaction, going through life with nothing worse than a tame inner bully is in the end more of a "lottery winner" than winning a multimillion-dollar lottery! In unfortunate contrast, most people—at least those who show up in my office anyway—are likely to be struggling with an, I'll call it, *taunting* inner bully at best, and a basically *tormenting* one at worst.

To recap, being on the receiving end of bullying types of physical acts of aggression, belittling statements, and nonverbal expressions of disapproval can create a negative internal echo that becomes the voice of the inner bully. The echo is created by either obvious acts of bullying (direct hits) or subtler negative communication (sneak attacks). Our inner bully tells us what we deserve or don't deserve and also tends to exaggerate any of our failures, whether they are real or imagined. The best way to handle our inner bully is to learn how to stand up to it, especially via the strategies to be presented in Chapters 7 and 8 (as I indicated back in the Introduction, please feel free at any time to jump ahead to any of them if you'd like, to get a feel for what some of those strategies are). By doing so, you will be able to bounce back more quickly when confronted with a blow to your self-Worth.

Exercise: Inner Echo, Inner Bully

Make a list of the "direct hits" you received while growing up that came from your mother or other female parental figure. Then make another indicating those you received from your father or father figure. Complete the same exercise for any "sneak attacks" you feel that you experienced at either or both ends. Then, rank the top three direct hits and sneak attacks overall, across both parents, that you feel have caused you the most distress or those that you believe have continued to affect you most up to this day. This can help you gain a clearer understanding of and ability to recognize your "inner echo" at work within you.

Chapter 3

Inner Agitation

MARLENE IS A THIRTY-NINE-YEAR-OLD WOMAN WITH two kids who is on the verge of divorce. Marlene loves her children dearly. One of them is mildly autistic and the other has ADHD. Both of her kids therefore present significant behavioral and emotional challenges to Marlene. In the process, this creates a good deal of daily stress for her. Complicating this stress is the fact that Marlene is a perfectionist. Therefore she ends up being very self-critical when she can't get one of her kids to be more cooperative or the house looks like "one big mess" to her.

On the marital front, the divorce proceedings have been gut-wrenching for two reasons. First, Marlene found out a few months ago that her husband, John, had been cheating on her. She had no inkling of this and therefore was blindsided by John's infidelity and betrayal. The second reason for Marlene's distress over her impending divorce is the considerable financial pressure she will be under once the divorce is final.

With regard to work, Marlene is a paralegal in a law firm. She generally enjoys her work but has a very demanding and moody boss. As Marlene puts it, "He typically has no clue about what it means to give credit where credit is due!" This aggravating attitude on her boss's part leaves Marlene with her stomach churning a good part of each workday.

Mark is a fifty-two-year-old, never-married owner of a graphic design business who is in the throes of a financial crisis due to his business falling off over the continuing depressing state of the economy. Mark wakes up most mornings feeling churned up inside and struggles to get out of bed. His thoughts are always racing, and he worries about the future throughout most of the day. Mark also has an ailing father who depends on Mark for both financial and physical assistance. Despite being a devoted son, he still resents being limited by the time and energy he has to give his father because it adversely affects his love life.

Mark is also distressed over some health issues. While none of these issues are life threatening, they still keep him preoccupied, if not obsessed. His frequent headaches and nightly insomnia are of particular concern to Mark. Nonetheless, while he does take some medications for these symptoms, Mark's high stress level keeps these symptoms alive and kicking, much to his frustration and dismay.

People like Marlene and Mark are leading lives filled with stress. Yet as I have emphasized to both Marlene and Mark over their course of treatment, probably half of their stress is brought on by their inner bully. After all, how else do you explain why these two caring, hardworking, devoted people are nonetheless convinced they're never doing well enough in their own eyes?

How does this combination of circumstantial stress and inner bully–induced, irrational self-condemnation leave Marlene and Mark feeling most of the time? To quote Marlene, "I almost always feel churned up inside, so it's really hard for me to relax, and I don't sleep well. Plus my blood pressure is high, and my stomach upsets me half the time, so it isn't easy at all for me to keep going day after day. Unfortunately, I have no choice!"

Chances are you do not need to have all of Marlene and Mark's life stresses to understand all their turmoil inside, negatively affecting both of them on a daily basis. For most people, any *one* of these stresses could very well get that "ogita" going, for example on the job front, in a marriage or other significant relationship, parenting, dealing with in-laws, or financial strain. If you have more than one of these stresses, chances are your churning will be multiplied commensurately.

Core Churning and Core Agitation

You are familiar no doubt with the word *agitation*. For most people, the word conjures up an image of someone who appears to be emotionally flying off the handle. From the person's irritated facial expression, distressed tone of voice, pressured speech, flailing arms, or constant pacing, it usually is clear from observation when someone appears to be in a state of agitation (or to bring in one of my favorite Yiddish words of my childhood, a state of "shpielkes.")

There is one important distinction I want to make. Agitation is the core *churning* inside during any intense negative emotion, not just anger and anxiety, but also, for example, guilt, hurt, jealously, frustration, or disappointment. Being agitat*ed*, on the other hand, refers to the observable, behavioral expressions of that agitation like the examples of out-of-control behaviors listed above.

Let me offer an analogy about core agitation. When you are churned up inside, your agitation can feel like the equivalent of being a shirt during the wash cycle in a washing machine. When you're extra churned up, it can feel more like you are being tossed around in the speeding spin cycle!

Agitation and Your Inner Bully

In order for anyone to function effectively in life, we all need a good source of energy. For example, anything such as food and drink, exercise, intellectual stimulation, fantasy, or laughter can all in different ways and different times provide us with a spark of energy. Well it's no different for your inner bully. It too needs a source of energy to function, and it has a very convenient source of negative energy, and that's your core agitation that is available to it every day.

Look at it this way. The stronger your core churning or agitation, the more upset and distressed you are likely to be. Regardless of the specific situational trigger at the moment, the more agitation you feel at a given moment, the more vulnerable you are to experiencing intense negative emotions. Again, these especially include emotions like anger, guilt, hurt, sadness, frustration, disappointment, and jealousy. Once these negative emotions rise to the surface and get channeled into self-sabotaging thoughts and actions, the more you can assume your inner bully is the energized "channeler." Once your inner bully has all this channeled agitation in its grasp, the more it can make a Marlene or Mark out of you, me, and everyone else!

As a side note, I always encourage my patients—not to mention remind *myself*-- to refrain from describing negative emotions in black and white terms. It is more helpful to express those words in the degree or intensity that you are experiencing them. Specifically, you have two options here. One is to distinguish them as mild, manageable, or overwhelming. The other is to rate their intensity on a rating scale, where 9-10 reflects an overwhelming amount of that emotion, 4-6 implies a manageable amount of that feeling, and anything below 3 represents only a mild amount of that emotion. Moving from black and white descriptions of feelings to gray-area descriptions allows you the opportunity to become more conscious of how you may in reality not be feeling an overwhelming amount of a particular emotion at all. Instead, you may come to the realization that the intensity of that emotion is actually quite manageable, if not relatively mild.

Also keep in mind that agitation can manifest on three levels: the *cognitive*, the *emotional*, and the *physical/somatic*. Cognitively, you've got two possibilities. On the one hand, you can experience a stream of obsessive negative thinking that can be quite unnerving. On the other hand, however, you may end up going the opposite route via thought blocking where you can't really think clearly at all about anything; call that "brain freeze" if you will. Emotionally, you can feel an intense amount of negative feelings rising to the surface, from anxiety to guilt to anger to jealousy. Finally, on a physical level, your agitation can manifest as stress-based health problems like insomnia, headaches, gastrointestinal disturbances, or high blood pressure.

Agitation and Psychological Disorders

Typically when people come to my office, they begin by telling me what is going on *clinically* that convinced them to set up an appointment. For most people seeking psychotherapy, it's virtually guaranteed they will characterize themselves as depressed, overly anxious, or both. Some people may also report symptoms of an obsessive-compulsive disorder (OCD), post-traumatic stress disorder (PTSD), attention deficit disorder (ADD/ADHD), or some kind of mood disorder. Some also seek help for addictions.

As you can see, there end up being quite a few different possible clinical problems with various presenting symptoms that cause people to seek professional help. All of them can have a behavioral component (for example, lack of motivation and social avoidance), an emotional component (for example, hurt and guilt), and/or a physiological component (for example, insomnia or headaches). All of them share an underlying "core" composed mainly of agitation.

When I am working with patients who tell me they are suffering from depression, anxiety attacks, OCD, an eating disorder, or some type of addiction, I tell them I will help manage their symptoms in part by helping them manage their core agitation. That way, the less agitation you have inside you, the less "fuel" your inner bully has available to create your distressing and self-sabotaging clinical symptoms. In light of that, if you want to get your clinical symptoms in check, you must get your agitation in check. Of course when say that I can hear many of you thinking, "Yeah right. A lot easier said than done!"

Agitation and "Tunnel Focus"

At one time or another, we all get worked up inside over various life circumstances. This can happen over something as relatively mundane as your favorite sports team losing a game (which to a crazy sports fan like me is never actually mundane), to more important circumstances like your financial situation, a big argument with a loved one, or health concerns. In all of these situations, when your core agitation kicks in, you are guaranteed to be unable to think or concentrate as clearly as when you are *not* in this state of agitation. More specifically, if your agitation level is relatively mild, chances are that the adverse effect on these cognitive capacities will be small and short-lived. In contrast, in a state of high agitation, you can feel as though the term "no-brainer" in this case means your brain has temporarily disappeared. In turn, this leads to a paradox, because when you can't concentrate clearly, you end up feeling more frustrated. Unfortunately, all that the frustration does is add to your core agitation and make it even harder to think and concentrate clearly. This leaves you with even further frustration. Round and round goes the vicious circle.

I use the term "tunnel focus" to describe the difficulty with focus and concentration we all experience at one time or another in a heightened state of agitation. Tunnel focus is not equivalent to tunnel *vision*. The latter refers of course to narrow-mindedness. Tunnel *focus*, on the other hand, refers to the automatic process that occurs when your core agitation level gets strong and your conscious mind basically enters a "tunnel." In that "tunnel," you are only able to focus on two things: (1) the fact that you are in a heightened state of agitation, and (2) the situational cause at that moment of your agitation.

Therefore, the problem that you are going to experience during states of tunnel focus is that you will be unable to consciously focus on how to get *out* of your "tunnel." So you end up being stuck—that is, trapped with your thoughts obsessively racing away or exactly the opposite when your thoughts are almost completely blocked (brain freeze). In the process, you are likely to experience a temporary but frustrating inhibiting of your, e.g., concentration, short-term memory, and capacity to laugh and have fun.

Hopefully though, sooner rather than later, you will be able to see light at the end of that tunnel since remaining in that tunnel will only feel dark indeed. Once you see some type of light, chances are you will become clear in your mind about some strategies for getting yourself out of the tunnel. These strategies can include meditating, journaling, walking or some other type of exercise, or asking for and getting a big hug. These activities gradually do get you out of that tunnel and into a more manageable state of agitation-- possibly even into a state of needed relaxation!

Agitation and Your Amygdala

The field of behavioral neuroscience has become a hot area of research and clinical application regarding the connection between human behavior and the brain's anatomy and functioning. I particular want to focus on the structure in the brain known as the *amygdala* (pronounced a-MIG-da-la). Research has established that this little piece of the brain plays a big role in states of agitation, which can manifest in either intense anxiety or anger. Also known as the "flight-fight" response, when your overall circumstantial stress level is high, you can assume your amygdala is firing away. The more your amygdala is firing away, the more vulnerable you become to the onset and persistence of agitation-induced tunnel focus. In turn, this temporarily renders the rational, executive thinking part of your brain, known as the *prefrontal cortex*, pretty useless. As behavioral neuroscientists describe it, the high-firing *amygdala* "hijacks" the prefrontal cortex. As a result of that hijacking, back into that tunnel you will go.

Then there's the part in the brain known as the *anterior cingulate gyrus*. This structure is hypothesized in some circles to be the seat of judgmental capacities. As behavioral neuroscience researcher and esteemed colleague Joel Weintraub suggests, the ACG may be the part of the brain that mediates self-judgment. Arguably then, when the ACG is overstimulated, it can result in impaired judgment in general, which in turn can manifest in excessive negative *self*-judgment—in other words, bring out your inner bully!

Putting this all together, you get the following chain of brain events. You do something that makes you very upset with yourself, such as losing your car keys, not speaking up to your boss, or forgetting your best friend's birthday. Your agitation level shoots up. The heightened agitation causes your amygdala and anterior cingulated gyrus to fire away, especially in the negative self-judgment direction. The fired-up amygdala hijacks your prefrontal cortex, leaving you in the throes of tunnel focus. In this state of negative self-judgment, your inner bully can overpower you. That's when you will need your "menu" of the type of agitation-reducing strategies listed above.

When Tunnel Focus Is a Good Thing

Sometimes tunnel focus is a true asset and not a major liability. The first advantageous type of tunnel focus can occur during deep states of meditation. As Andrew Newberg underscores in his intriguing book *How God Changes the Brain*, in deep meditative states, you can experience a wonderfully peaceful and spiritually penetrating form of tunnel focus, which you might call being in a "zone." This zone state is the opposite experience of unnerving, self-sabotaging tunnel focus created by a heightened state of agitation. In other words, if you are in the midst of tunnel focus that accompanies a contemplative meditative state, then this tunnel is already filled with lots of light, a light that can have a spiritual underpinning if you choose to experience it that way.

Even more importantly on a day to day basis, tunnel focus is much more a positive than a negative when it comes to the cognitive coping style of *compartmentalization*. Specifically, someone who tends to compartmentalize their stress and agitation is able most of the time to automatically place it in a mental "compartment" in the mind. Once it's in there, the compartment immediately gets shut tightly—out of sight, out of mind. Of course, most people cannot do this all of the time. There certainly are occasions when a compartmentalizer joins the ranks of an average worrywart, also known as an *obsessor* For the most part, though, that's the exception rather than the rule for your average compartmentalizer. Unfortunately, this is not the case for obsessors, who typically are stuck with their obsessive worrying.

In a nutshell, in a stressful state, if you are caught in a tunnel of either obsessing on the agitation itself or going blank, it is virtually guaranteed you are going to remain mired in a high level of agitation longer than you would like to be. On the other hand, suppose as your agitation is rising up to the surface, you are cognitively able to interrupt the agitation. If that happens, you will be much less likely to enter that tunnel than if you obsess. This makes me wish there was a special type of blood transfusion for transferring the blood of a compartmentalizer to an obsessor. I figure if I invested in the company that produced a device like this I could make a mint!

Agitation, Guilt, Embarrassment, and Shame

As mentioned previously, patients come to see me or one of my colleagues with various clinical problems. However, as quickly as possible, I move off clinical diagnoses and onto the individual's core agitation and its self-sabotaging manifestations in his/her life. Once again, "deserve" and "failure" issues become a central part of the treatment focus for cutting down on that self-sabotage.

I break the "d-word" and "f-word" down for my patients into three main emotional components: *guilt, embarrassment,* and *shame.* The creation of these three painful emotions represents a huge victory for your inner bully over your core self-Worth. The more intensely you feel one or more of these emotions inside you, the higher your core agitation level will be. This is, of course, just what this (witch) doctor, your inner bully, ordered.

You are no doubt familiar with the words guilt, embarrassment, and shame. Unfortunately, you may also be quite familiar with what these emotions can do to you when they take control of you. If the intensity of your overall agitation remains relatively low, only a minor amount of any of these three negative emotions are likely to build over time. However, the stronger your agitation, the much more vulnerable you are to experiencing these three feelings to an intense degree.

From my vantage point, the distinction among these three distressing emotions is by no means always clear. Guilt will be defined here as doing something or not doing something specific that makes you feel "bad" about yourself in your own eyes.

From that definitional standpoint, guilt can have psychologically harmful effects on anyone. Still, the feeling is in a sense limited to the situational/behavioral trigger for it. However, there is plenty of room for that "limited" guilt to sooner or later overwhelm you. That's especially the case if the context of your guilt is an important one to you, for example, not hurting people you care about, not working as hard as you usually do on tasks or projects, or not living up to your generally high standards and expectations for yourself in school.

As for *embarrassment*, the key here is not just that you feel deep down that what you did was "bad." Worse, it ends up making you feel like you also look bad in the eyes of people around you, whose opinions and judgment may count a lot to you—oftentimes too much. Embarrassment takes guilt and switches the focus off of your own reactions and self-judgments about doing something "bad" and puts it onto *others'* reactions and judgments to it.

Then there's *shame* or, as author John Bradshaw coined the term decades ago, "toxic" shame, especially when the shame is chronic. Shame cuts deeper into your emotional core than do guilt or embarrassment. Shame basically takes guilt and embarrassment and combines them into a "stew." Then it becomes not just feeling that something you did was "bad," in your own eyes or the eyes of others. It's deeper than that: it's the feeling that *you* are bad, bad at the core. Clinically speaking, shame leaves you more vulnerable to episodes of clinical depression and strong social anxiety than guilt or embarrassment.

Certainly, shame is toxic because in addition to the ways it can adversely affect you clinically, it can also sap your self-confidence in multiple life areas. It can leave you feeling like no one could possibly like or respect you, much less truly love you. Yet the irony is that no matter how much core shame you may have and how much negative projecting you may do, you can still be liked, loved, and respected in enough ways by people who really matter to you anyway. In other words, shame can interfere with your ability to see the forest through the trees, especially regarding what is *right and good* about you!

Fortunately, though, all is not lost in the battle to tackle any of your major unresolved guilt, embarrassments, or even toxic shame. In Chapters 7 through 9, you will be presented a toolbox of ways to stand up to your inner bully's attempts to make you feel deserving of irrational guilt, embarrassment, and toxic shame.

In summary, agitation is defined as a core churning inside that can manifest to varying intensities emotionally, behaviorally, and somatically. The higher the level and the longer lasting the agitation, the more susceptible you are to psychological problems like depression and anxiety attacks. High levels of agitation trigger tunnel focus, which interferes with concentration, short-term memory, and the capacity to laugh and have fun. Finally, behavioral neuroscience demonstrates that agitation level is connected to interrelated functioning of specific parts of the brain.

Ok, time for another round of exercises.

Exercises

Choose three situations in your life that create the strongest churning or agitation inside you. If you prefer, you are welcome to list more. For each type of situational agitation listed, focus on how it manifested itself cognitively, emotionally, and physically. You will probably notice that some situations affect you only emotionally whereas others may affect you in all three of those areas. What feelings typically come up for you when your agitation level is high? Would you rate them right up there as a ten or are any of them at a more manageable level like a six? Later exercises will build on this one to help you gain control over these three areas of agitation-based churning inside.

Chapter 4

Betrayal

"WHEN YOU BETRAY SOMEONE YOU ALSO betray yourself." —
Isaac Bashevis Singer

"Betrayal is about learning not to idealize external sources."
—Linda Talley

"Betrayal and deceit are two qualities that create a sense of awakening from a nightmare only to discover that the reality is in fact not a dream. Betrayal and deceit always have a very negative effect on the relationship between the betrayer and the betrayed. The scar of betrayal may never be erased. It takes a long period of time to rebuild trust between the betrayer and the betrayed."—Anonymous

Experiencing a betrayal by someone important to you can be as disturbing if not demoralizing an experience as any in life. The betrayal can be outright traumatizing to you if you consider it to be a major betrayal and if it's carried out by someone important to you. You are also likely to experience the strongest sense of betrayal when it involves a context in your life that is an important one, for example, your primary romantic relationship, your job, or your friendships. A strong sense of betrayal is also more likely if the value involved is high priority to you, such as honesty, ambitiousness, or financial sensibility.

Take Harry for instance. Over the previous two years, Harry did not have much going right for him. First he found out through a friend's spouse that Martha, his wife of nineteen years, had been unfaithful to him for months. Harry was devastated, especially because he had no clue at all of her infidelity. Adding to that indiscretion, three months later, Harry's older teenager, Barry, was arrested for breaking and entering a house with a couple of friends. Harry was caught by surprise by this shocking turn of events as he had always viewed Barry as "your basic good kid."

That wasn't the end of it for poor Harry. One day, Martha called him at work to tell him that his beloved primary care physician of over thirty years had his license suspended because he had been charged with excessive distribution of painkillers to many of his patients. Harry's faith in his doctor was such that even when he and Martha moved two hours away, he continued to see "my man Doc" for all medical visits.

Then, one day at the office, Harry's boss announced at a staff meeting that two staff members would be promoted by the end of the year. Feeling assured he would be granted one of the promotions, it burned Harry up to hear that he in fact was *neither* of the two.

Last but not least, Harry's father died suddenly of a stroke, which left Harry feeling he had lost his "rock." Of course, Harry knew for years that his "rock" was overweight and smoked, which upset Harry to no end and which he knew contributed significantly to his father's demise. Three months before he died, his father had "promised" Harry that he would change his lifestyle drastically, and in fact he had been doing that more than he had for as long as Harry could remember. This left Harry with some optimism about his Dad's health, optimism that sadly turned out to be misguided.

What's the moral of the story here? Granted, it's unlikely that anyone would experience a bombardment of unrelated betrayals like poor Harry did in such a relatively short time. But what beleaguered Harry can readily attest to is that betrayal can occur at any time in any important context of your life.

Once you discover you've been betrayed, chances are you will experience a two-sided coin of intense emotional reaction in the gut. Either consciously or subconsciously, one side of that emotional coin is deep *hurt* while the other is *anger* if not outright rage. The chances also are that these two betrayal-triggered feelings will fluctuate as to which predominates inside you at any given time. Therefore, on one day or many days in a row, you may be aware of mainly being very sad or hurt over the betrayal. Yet on another day, you are likely to mainly feel angry and resentful of the betrayer. That fluctuation between hurt and resentment may even make you look like a betrayal-filled version of a Dr. Jekyll/Mr. Hyde. You need to know that both of these sets of feelings are perfectly human and normal under the circumstances of betrayal.

"Betrayal Trauma"

University of Oregon psychologist Jennifer Fryes coined the term *betrayal trauma* mainly in regard to the trauma of being abused as a child. Childhood abuse is of course one of the worst forms of betrayal possible. After all, what child could ever imagine being born into a world in which either of their parents would mistreat him/her in such a reprehensible and unwarranted manner? In the process, they end up doing the exact opposite of providing that child with a comforting, loving, and guidance-filled parent—something I firmly believe every child has the right to expect from both parents from the moment that the child enters into the world.

Betrayal: A Working Definition

Allow me to present the working definition of betrayal as the blueprint for where things will head in the remainder of this chapter. As you will see, the definition is by no means limited to prototypic categories of betrayal, that is, abuse in childhood and relationship infidelity in adulthood. The general definition of betrayal to be used is this: any major feeling of letdown by someone important to you, based on what you believed you had the right to believe they would never do to you. I must interject here that there is room in all of us to experience betrayals as being on a continuum from relatively minor (for example, forgetting a loved one's birthday) right through to truly major (again, especially abuse and infidelity).

Given this definition of betrayal, I assume it's clear how it can apply to betrayals above and beyond abuse and adult relationship infidelity. Harry certainly is a prime example of multiple betrayals. Here are some more examples. Suppose your significant other gave you the distinct impression early on in the relationship that he/she was ambitious and driven regarding job or career direction. But then as the next year or two go by, you see that in truth he/she allows the stress and anxiety they experience at times to *undermine* that ambition and drive. That individual is likely to end up in the throes of inner bully–induced self-sabotage and may for example jump from one job to another, taking extended periods of downtime between each almost inevitable job termination.

Or suppose you discover that a significant romantic partner, a parent, or one of your children has hidden something important from you, something they assumed would upset you a great deal if you found out about it. For example, you may discover that the individual has had a problem with substance abuse or excessive gambling. This blind-siding of you regarding a previously hidden or denied addiction can leave you feeling betrayed enough to want to put a halt to the relationship, temporarily if not permanently.

Betrayal and Feelings of Injustice

For those of you who are into astrology, I am letting you know I am a Libra, but I am not telling you this because *I'm* into astrology. I tell you this only because the irony to me is that while I am not into astrology, the astrologically defined meaning of the sign of Libra—someone for whom the scales of justice are a high priority in life—fits me to a tee.

The perception and experience that you have been betrayed certainly can feel like a major injustice has been perpetrated against you. The injustice could have come from the same sources as any other betrayal, that is, a parent, a significant other, a boss, a friend, or a teacher. For example, if you felt that one of your siblings definitely was favored over you while you were growing up, that can feel quite unjust. That's because it can feel perfectly reasonable for you to expect that your parents will love each of their children the same and treat them equally. When your perception of your upbringing differs from that, chances are you will feel betrayed whether or not you know it consciously. Meanwhile, it is virtually guaranteed that this perception of yours would be emphatically denied by your parents should you choose to confront them about it. This denial will likely not be believable to you, which in turn can keep the feeling of betrayal alive and kicking.

(Arguably) The Five Worst Possible Betrayals

From my vantage point, of all the ways and contexts in which betrayal can be experienced, there are five that are likely to be the most psychologically harmful to anyone on the receiving end. These are infidelity, abuse, neglect, abandonment, and hypocrisy.

With regard to *infidelity*, having a romantic partner betray you by being unfaithful is virtually guaranteed to create a gut-wrenching feeling of betrayal. This type of betrayal can of course hurt deeply and possibly permanently. There is also a strong possibility that trust will never be rebuilt. Hence the chances are the relationship will be significantly damaged, temporarily if not permanently.

Concerning *abuse*, there essentially are three types: physical, sexual, and mental/emotional. All can involve either a single isolated incident or an ongoing pattern. A single incident of any of these acts is injustice enough and a betrayal unto itself. Multiple acts of one or a combination of these types of abuse can add up to a much bigger injustice and therefore even a bigger sense of being betrayed, as was the case with Harry.

When it comes to emotional abuse, this basically involves the pattern of "direct hit" and/or "sneak attack" communications from your inner bully previously discussed in chapter 2. This combination of strong feelings of injustice and intense emotions of betrayal are the likely emotional outcome of mental/emotional abuse. I encourage you to also keep in mind that as psychologically harmful as acts of physical or sexual abuse can be for the victim, mental/emotional abuse can cut even deeper into an abused person's psyche and soul. Yes, physical abuse can leave a lasting scar, at times literally. Yes, sexual abuse can create intimacy problems for the victim. However, in terms of deep, pervasive, and lasting psychological harm especially regarding your core self-Worth, mental abuse can take that self-Worth and crumble it even more than the other two types of abuse. And the worst-case scenario, God forbid, is being subjected to all three!

Then there's *neglect*. Neglect can occur on any of the following fronts and to varying degrees: material things, affection, attention, or amount of time spent with you. It's likely that feeling neglected materially will not affect you as negatively as feeling neglected in either of the other three areas. If you feel you truly lacked affection or time spent with family during your growing years, the chances are the hurt you may have resultingly experienced runs deep. This can in turn leave you feeling deep down that you aren't worth much as a person. At the same time, it can also lead you to believe that the world basically "owes" you to make up for the neglect to which you were subjected. The more you feel that way though, the greater the likelihood is that you will become bitter and feel alienated--which your inner bully would love you to feel!

Anyone can feel neglected in an *absolute* sense (that is, you and you alone were neglected), but you can also feel neglected in a *relative* sense (that is, compared to someone else such as a family member or friend, particularly in the developing years). Yet as noted above, if you accuse the seemingly favorite-playing parent, relative, or teacher of neglecting you, your accusation may be met with a denial along the lines of "What are talking about? That's absolutely crazy!"

Abandonment can also be emotionally traumatizing. Suppose one of your parents or another significant person in your life—for whatever indefensible reason—leaves your world for months if not many years. When this traumatizing event occurs, you may enter adult life feeling pretty much the same thing inside as you would from being neglected, that is, worthless and unlovable as a person. However, it is extremely important that you be as mindful as you can that those harsh self-judgments are only according to your inner bully's "truth"—and hence not the *real* truth. The real truth is that, in spite of being neglected or abandoned, you are every bit as lovable and worthwhile as anyone else!

You may ask what happens when you feel that only *one* of your parents significantly neglected or outright abandoned you and not the other one? Unfortunately, my professional experience has been that no matter how much that parent (or other relatives for that matter) may have treated you in a very attentive and affectionate manner, you are still likely to enter adult life highly vulnerable to feeling rejected and/or unlovable. This pattern of negative psychological effect on a growing child of unhealthy parenting by one parent is something I see evidence of over and over. Although having one loving parent or adult figure certainly helps the situation—potentially a great deal in fact--the positive psychological effect that this person can have on you can unfortunately be outweighed by the negative messages you may receive from the neglectful/abandonning in your life. Let me underscore here though that what can also be quite beneficial to a child who feels neglected or outright abandoned is to have some type of *mentor* in your life. Be it another relative, a coach, a teacher, or a clergyman, the ongoingly supportive and guiding hand of a mentor can potentially go a long way to compensating for the psychologically undermining effects a neglectful/abandoning parent may have.

Last but not least is the betrayal of *hypocrisy*. The essential ingredient here is the infamous "Do as I say, not as I do!" communication. It does not matter one bit whether this message is presented explicitly or implicitly. It also does not matter whether this hypocritical message is being presented by a parent, teacher, coach, or clergyman. Regardless of who the hypocrite is, all that matters is when that individual does not do what he/she tells *you* to do, in my eyes that's a form of injustice and betrayal rolled into one.

Two quick examples of this type of hypocrisy follow. A parent orders you to squelch your anger at all times, but then at times he/she has their own temper tantrums. Needless to say, that's not just a lousy role-model in this particular area; it's outright hypocrisy. Another especially distressing example would be the stories we all hear at times about the few conscienceless clergymen who preach devotion to God while at the same time proceeding to defile Him through ungodly behavior toward young people. Taking both examples together, you can end up feeling like the line from the old Prestone antifreeze commercial, "If you can't trust Prestone, who *can* you trust?" Showing my age here on this last example, but you get the point.

Overall, I assume it's clear that examples of hypocrisy like these boil down to the opposite of the directive "Practice what you preach!" Under these circumstances, credibility is only established or reestablished when the hypocritical person takes it upon himself to change and become a role model of the message "Do as I say *and as I DO!*"

As a little postscript, *religious/spiritual* betrayal is another type of betrayal that can feel like a major injustice unto itself. This one has to do with God, assuming you have or had a strong spiritual belief in God. If that's the case, then chances are you can feel betrayed by God when something tragic happens to you or a loved one. For example, suppose you have a significant other or close relative whom you see as a deeply caring and giving person, who is much beloved by most people who know him/her. Then suppose one day this same special person is attacked and viciously beaten by a gang of hoodlums. If you believe that God should never have allowed something that terrible to happen, then there is a real possibility that consciously or subconsciously, you will feel betrayed by a God who is supposed to be all powerful, who always triumphs over evil, etc., etc. The same thing can occur when we discover that a child has cancer, when a natural disaster has occurred, or when millions of people were killed by an evil, subhuman individual. "How can a supposedly loving God allow any of these awful things to happen?" you may painfully wonder, with all of the depth of feeling of betrayal that you are virtually guaranteed to feel when you ask that. Especially for ye of faith, feeling betrayed by God is likely need I tell you to leave ye feeling a major loss of that faith.

Betrayal and Bitterness

Norma is a forty-five- year-old divorced woman who finally ended an unhappy and unfulfilling marriage of twelve years. Both of Norma's parents are still alive and are very much the dictionary definition of the proverbial "Bickersons." The older of Norma's two teenagers is an exceptionally bright but very defiant young man. The younger one stays to herself and refuses to be sociable, spending most of her time playing video games or texting virtually nonstop with her only friend, Tammy. Norma's husband was emotionally abusive to her and, in Norma's eyes, financially "screwed" her over in the divorce settlement. Mainly as a result of that "screwing over" and with very little financial help offered by her parents, Norma was forced to work two jobs just to make ends meet.

In light of these distressing, frustrating circumstances facing Norma daily, I'm sure it comes as no surprise to learn that Norma was often perceived as a "negative person." Specifically, she often came across as overcritical and undercrediting of people. She complained about many aspects of her life and was often short-tempered and irritable. As a result of these alienating tendencies, Norma, as one would expect, had few real friends.

Given this picture of Norma, I think it's safe to say she sounds like she is filled with *bitterness*, a perpetual Mrs. Scrooge you might say. This is reflected in Norma's basic attitude of "I want everyone to know how angry and frustrated I am with my life. As a result, I am announcing that the world rid me of my miserable circumstances!"

In the process, someone like Norma is going to create an emotional double whammy of self-sabotage for herself. Most likely, Norma will not win any popularity contests, and very few people in her life will have much incentive to assist her in her quest to get some justice in her lifetime.

There is an analogy I often use for bitterness: "psychological quicksand." In real quicksand, once you sink into it, forget it, you'll be sinking all the way down to the bottom and will die. In the "quicksand" of bitterness however, any bitter person can sink down into the "muck," but this sinking involves your head always remaining on the surface while the rest of your body remains submerged. In other words, although you are trapped in this muck, you can still "use your head"—literally and figuratively—to prevent yourself from drowning from all of the complaints and condemnations you may continue to experience inside from an initial betrayal and then beyond.

Furthermore, in real quicksand, if a sinking person reaches up from the muck with his/her arm raised, it's clear the person desperately wants to be pulled out. In the quicksand of bitterness, however, when a bitter person appears to be reaching up with an arm, he/she is not reaching out for assistance. Instead, the person is trying to pull you *in* with them! That gives the bitter person the opportunity to experience a "bond" with you. It is an emotional bond that really is not a bond at all, but rather the essence of the old "misery loves company" notion.

Please keep in mind here though that I'm not saying that someone who is bitter never enjoys life at all. Certainly there are times when the bitterness itself—rather than the person—sinks down below the surface. In those moments, someone who is bitter certainly can appear to be not be miserable at all, and, e.g., enjoy time with people, have fun, do well on their job, or pursue a passionate hobby. There are even times when someone in the throes of bitterness can actually show a tender side, as for example when in the company of a child. In fact, I recall seeing a photo in a book in an old bookstore of a touching-looking photograph of Adolph Hitler with a cherubic young child perched on his lap. The child is smiling gaily, appearing to be perfectly content sitting on the lap of this evil mass murderer!

The problem with bitter people is that it doesn't take much to get their bitter dark side going. Any upsets occurring around them can bring their bitterness to the surface, in essence causing Dr. Jekyll to transform into Mr. Hyde. In fact, it might take little more than an encounter with someone who physically reminds the bitter person of the person who betrayed him/her. It may even be a scene from a TV show or a movie that connects in some distressing way to the type of betrayal that occurred to the bitter person. No matter what at the moment actually triggers it, the effect can be a zero to a hundred appearance of a bitterness "attack."

Bitterness, Agitation, and Betrayal

When anyone feels betrayed, lots of core agitation and churning begins to accumulate inside you. This can keep you in a pretty continuous state of turmoil. This turmoil can then be used by your inner bully to get you to "stay the course" on the path of bitterness. In turn, this allows your inner bully the "pleasure" of potentially jeopardizing some of the most valuable relationships in your life.

If your inner bully isn't causing enough trouble already, there still is one more piece of the puzzle to put on the table. In my experience, anyone who is filled with the agitation of bitterness is virtually guaranteed to have two accompanying issues. One is the tendency to be *grudge-holding*. In that stae of being, the perceived betrayor can pay the price indefinitely, even if he/she makes amends in some way to the betrayee.

The other bitterness-related issue that can arise is *jealousy*. The jealousy can be related to others' material possessions, although in my view, that's more *envy* than jealousy. From my vantage point, jealousy is when the issue is on a more personal level, such as having an acquaintance you see as more outgoing than you are, or knowing someone who has a relationship with the love of his/her life and you don't.

When you are mired in betrayal-induced agitation, you are likely to be prone to major jealousy attacks. It does not matter one iota whether you openly acknowledge your jealousy or not. Like a psychological virus, jealousy can lay dormant inside for quite some time. When it rises up to the surface, however, it can steer anyone down one of two unfortunate paths. The chances are you will either begin to display a pattern of unwarranted, unprovoked attacks on other people, or you can end up in a pattern of avoiding and withdrawing from people, at least temporarily anyway. Either of these options becomes another sabotaging victory for your inner bully. This is just what happened to our distraught protagonist Norma: she ended up with few real friends and little happiness in her life.

As a little postscript here though, there is a difference between a manageable amount of jealousy everyone experiences at one time or another versus a *pathological* amount of jealousy. In a nutshell, when your jealousy is in a manageable category (a rating of a 5 or a 6 on a 1 to 10 scale, where 10 is extreme jealousy), your jealousy most likely will not be intense enough to cause you to sabotage relationships and undercut your self-worth to any significant degree.

Pathological jealousy (a 9 or 10 on the scale), on the other hand, is likely to be a much bigger "deal-breaker." Pathological jealousy can break down most of your significant relationships and severely damage your core self-worth. When you really think about it, this is a form of betraying *yourself*, especially if you do something you believed you would never do to yourself. This self-betrayal can in turn create even more agitation, which then feeds your jealousy more and so continues the destructive cycle. Meanwhile, your inner bully is cackling away at your misfortune from the sidelines.

After years of pondering the matter, I have come to the conclusion that the combination of pathological jealousy, feelings of alienation, and core feelings of betrayal from childhood add up to being the proverbial "root of all evil," which can result in jealousy of money, wealth, material possessions, love, and success.

This inner bully–induced, self-sabotaging emotion can especially arise, as noted previously, from deep-rooted feelings that you were severely deprived in some important ways particularly with regard to basic love and affection.

Additionally, pathological jealousy will most likely lead to outright evil actions when it eats away at a person's *conscience*. The downhill chain of internal psychological events that culminate into creating evil basically works like this: Betrayal→ Bitterness→ Pathological Jealousy→ Loss of Conscience→ Evil Actions. Combined with chronic low self-worth and lots of core insecurity, this leaves plenty of room for someone to become a certified member of the traumatizing "evil club."

Evil Versus the Inner Bully

When I first began sharing my perspective about evil and the inner bully with some of my patients many years ago, an interesting thing sometimes happened. A few of my patients, particularly the most religious of Catholics and Christians, would tell me that my description of the inner bully sounded to them like the proverbial notion of the devil, and the classic characterization of the devil on one shoulder and an angel on the other.

Intrigued, I found myself eventually reaching a perspective on the subject of evil that took a different direction than I had ever considered. Given the fact that I view the inner bully as another, separate, inner force of evil too, my thoughts about these two different-named forces led to making the following distinction. The "devil" force is the term I use to characterize evil actions intentionally directed at *other* people, actions that clearly reflect a lack of conscience. On the other hand, the inner bully force reflects those thoughts and actions that are *self*-directed and *self*-sabotaging.

Consider the following paradox. If someone engages in evil toward other people, it would appear that they have almost no inner bully at all. In other words, those who intentionally do evil toward others are not the least bit caught up in what that does to their own self-Worth. Nor are they suffering from any pangs of human and circumstantially appropriate guilt. On the other hand, the chances that those who live with a tough inner bully will likely have a hard time emotionally coping with hurting anyone intentionally (except maybe in self-defense) because of the potentially *intense* guilt they may experience.

Moving to the "good force" side of the coin,, feel free to decide on a name to give to that positive, i.e., self-worth-building force isnide. For example, you might label this force God, the Higher Power, or Spirit. Or you could name it after a guardian angel. I personally choose to label my positive/angel force as God, but that's just my own choice. In the end, what matters most is that you view the positive force within you as a counterforce to the both the devil and inner bully forces.

Healing from Betrayal

Last but not least on the complicated subjects of betrayal and bitterness, how do we try to emotionally *heal* from betrayal? In many instances, when it comes to betrayal, the proverbial "time heals all wounds" notion ends up being just a cliché, because the unfortunate truth is that the passage of time by itself guarantees not a thing when it comes to healing from the wounds of betrayal.

I know I speak from personal and not just professional experience when I say that certain betrayals never fully heal, especially the ones that come from parents or romantic significant others. Still, if you are going to at least *try* to heal, you will need a "menu" of healing options. This menu should include options for getting comfort, giving to others, allowing moments of tears as well as moments of private angry venting, and pursuing passions. You also need to make sure to get in a few laughs whenever possible. After all, to quote Sheldon Kopp from his now semi-ancient but still quite meaningful book *If You Meet the Buddha on the Road, Kill Him*, "laughter is the sound of freedom." If you are mired in the "quicksand" of bitterness, how can you possibly feel free enough to laugh and have fun? Unfortunately, the less you laugh, the more your inner bully gets to laugh at you. Fortunately, the more *you* laugh, the less pleasure your inner bully gets to experience. In these situations, you end up getting the *last* laugh!

In sum, betrayal is any significant feeling of hurt and let down caused by a loved one's or other important person's actions that went contrary to your belief that they would never hurt you in the way that they have. The five worst betrayals (arguably) are infidelity, abuse, neglect, abandonment, and hypocrisy. Over time, betrayal if not checked can lead you to sink into "psychological quicksand," otherwise known as bitterness. Lastly, bitterness can grow under the power of our two negative forces: the devil and the inner bully.

The "Two-Way Street" of Betrayal

Before wrapping up this chapter with an exercise, it is very important that I offer you a balanced perspective on the subject of betrayal. What I mean by balanced perspective is simply this. On the one hand, you may be clear how you feel betrayed by someone important to you, and that's that. On the other hand, it may not occur to you to consider how that person feels betrayed in some way by *you!* In another words, betrayal can be a two-way street, whether either of you intended it to be that way or not.

Let me immediately add the following on the subject of two-way betrayal. Part of the healing process for you can be to, for a moment, step out of your agitation-filled focus on how you were betrayed by that person and go ahead and ask then if they felt betrayed in some way by *you.* Suppose that person tells you they feel betrayed by you along any of the same five lines presented above that you may be feeling towards them. At that point, two possible things could occur. On the one hand, you could disregard what he/she just told you as something you don't see as true at all and that's that. If that happens, you should still stick with your healing "menu."

On the other hand, you could look within yourself at the possibility that there really *has* been a two-way street of betrayal here. If you do that, then you open yourself and the other person to the possibility of some mutually healing *dialogue*. Dialogue in which you both make sure to listen to the other person's perspective and not just present your own, trying in the process to control your likely posture that *only you* are the one who has been betrayed here! Should you both become open to that possibility (slowly but surely), that can in turn potentially do wonders for your own personal healing from betrayal at minimum, and help you rebuild the relationship should you both choose to do that at maximum. This can especially come from making a commitment to each other to work on making amends to each other. Much more on making amends in a later chapter.

Now to an exercise.

Exercise

1) Make a list of the three most psychologically distressing betrayals you feel you have experienced over your lifetime.

2) For each betrayal, write down what negative emotions were triggered by it., especially hurt and anger.

3) Rate how intense each of these and any other emotions were for you on a 1-to-10 scale, where 1 = very mild, 10 = extremely intense). Approximately how long do you feel it took you for each betrayal's emotions to pass—if it ever has at all?

4) For those betrayals that were easier to get over, ask yourself what was different about those versus the ones that

were not as easy to get past. Is there something you did to lessen the impact of those betrayals? Based on this information, can you think of ways you can lower the intensity of your negative feelings caused by the more extreme betrayals?

5) Turning the tables around, who in your life has accused you of betraying them? In what way(s)? Do you feel the relationship between the two of you has been harmed in a significant if not irrevocable way? If not, how have you managed to heal together?

Chapter 5

Addiction to Self-Rebellion

Jennifer and Bill are sitting over dinner in a restaurant on a Friday night. Innocently and pleasantly enough, Bill asks Jennifer how her week went. Jennifer glares at Bill as though he's just asked her the most antagonizing, inflammatory question he could have come up with at that moment. "You want to know how my week was, Bill? I mean, do you *really* want to know how my week went?" she rhetorically but vehemently began. "I'll tell you how it went. It was terrible. I just couldn't do anything right for goodness sakes!"

Treading lightly, Bill encouraged Jennifer to "go ahead and lay it on me." Jennifer proceeded to reel off the following litany of events of her week. "Well, it started on Monday and then went downhill from there each day. On Monday, I missed a deadline my boss gave me because I kept procrastinating on the project I had to get done. On Tuesday, I was supposed to go to my nephew's recital after school, but I totally forgot about it. He was really disappointed I didn't come. Then on Wednesday,

I knew I shouldn't have done it but I went to a wine-tasting event and drank too much. Then I drove home by myself anyway. Yesterday, when I know I really should be sticking with my diet, I pretty much gorged myself all day. Plus, I haven't exercised at all in about two weeks. Then there is today. I know you've asked me to not text my old boyfriend John anymore. I'm really sorry, but the truth is we texted back and forth for about ten minutes this afternoon. I know I definitely shouldn't have done that. I really keep messing things up, Bill, don't I?"

As you can imagine, especially with that last little piece, Bill became quite upset with Jen. He glared at her from across the table and announced, "You sure do, babe—big time!"

As you can tell from her tirade, Jennifer has been on a "negative roll" for the past week. In the process, she has become the dictionary definition of a "self-saboteur." In each of the scenarios she recounted to Bill, Jennifer did something she knew she should not have done. From missing a deadline, to forgetting her nephew's recital, to drinking too much alcohol, to going way off her diet, to doing something that left Bill feeling betrayed by her, Jennifer kept doing the opposite of what was in her best interest to do. In theory, by reminding herself over and over what she should or shouldn't do in each of those situations, it was Jennifer's intent to motivate herself to do what was right in each situation. The fact is, Jennifer kept right on doing the opposite of the right thing.

Let me sum up what I mean here by doing something that is "in your best interest." In a nutshell, when you do something that fits that description, you are doing something that gratifies you and increases your self-Respect. For beleaguered Jennifer, this would have specifically translated into making her work deadlines, attending her nephew's recital, controlling her drinking, monitoring her food intake, and not texting an ex-boyfriend.

The term I like to use to describe the tendency to do the opposite of what is in our best interest is *self-rebellion*. I'm not using the word "rebellion" in the usual dictionary sense of the word, in terms of defying some authority figure. Instead, rebellion is being defined as doing something against one main "authority figure," *yourself*. In the classic movie *Rebel Without a Cause* starring the iconic James Dean, the main character, Jimmy Stark, makes a career out of rebelling mainly for the sake of rebelling. In other words, rebellion itself is his "raison d'être," no matter what the outcome of the rebellion may be. Viewed from that perspective, Stark's "causeless" rebellion fits the *dictionary* definition of rebellion more than my definition. In the latter case, though, a parallel here is that self-rebellion does in fact have a "cause." Unfortunately, though, it's a very negative cause, *self-sabotage*. It's a subconsciously driven self-sabotage, with the "driver" being— guess who--your inner bully.

The "Tyranny of the Shoulds"

Many moons ago, a colleague of mine recommended I read a book by psychoanalyst Dr. Karen Horney entitled *Neurosis and Human Growth*. In this somewhat esoteric yet intellectually stimulating book, Horney included a chapter intriguingly entitled

"The Tyranny of the Shoulds." Horney's basic point was that the use of "shoulds" and their cousins, the "supposed to's," can create a psychological tyranny of sorts inside you in terms of a self-sabotage backlash. More specifically, Horney's argument was that the more you tell yourself what you should or shouldn't do but you nonetheless go right ahead and do the opposite anyway, you end up in the process "tyrannizing" yourself. While the use of the term "tyranny" may feel a bit overdramatic in this context, doing the opposite of what's in your best interest is nonetheless likely to create a twofold psychological backlash—mainly in terms of guilt and loss of self-Respect. These in fact were the two distressing core emotions experienced by beleaguered Jennifer.

Shoulds and the "Two-Part Cognitive Split"

In honor of Dr. Horney's invaluable insight into the self-sabotaging world of the "shoulds," I want to share with you something that happened one day in my office. I was talking with a patient, Danielle, about her situational proneness to self-sabotage. Suddenly, Danielle began to sound like she was giving herself one heck of a self-critical lecture. As best as I remember it, Danielle cried out, "You know what I feel like saying to my-self, Doc? I really want to just say to myself, 'Danielle, you really should face once and for all that you are one big screwup. You almost never listen to your own advice or to anyone else's for that matter. You really should get your head examined!'"

At that moment during Danielle's blistering assessment of herself, a lightbulb went on in my mind. It struck me that Danielle was talking to herself like a *lecturing parent* would. Danielle was both the finger-pointing lecturer as well as the distressed recipient of the lecture. Then in the next moment, I reminded myself that too many of Danielle's actions in her daily life were adolescent rather than adult. Putting two and two together, you get what I'm going to call the should-triggered "two-part cognitive split." This is a split in your conscious mind that occurs almost instantaneously whenever you start doing something a colleague of mine once called (pardon a bit of off-coloredness here) "shoulding" on yourself.

It works like this. As soon as you start the "shoulding" process—whatever its content or focus may be—you are automatically speaking to yourself as though you are that lecturing parent to which I just alluded. For example, suppose you keep telling yourself you really should go to the doctor to have him/her check that mole that's been on your back for a while now. As soon as those "should" words enter your mind, you can assume your finger-pointing "lecturing parent" is in control of you. This is what I'm referring to as "cognitive split number one." Immediately though after you split into being a lecturing parent toward yourself, another part of your subconscious steps up to the plate. This part basically reacts to the "lecturing parent" with something along the lines of "Hey, don't tell me what I should or shouldn't do. You sound like a lecturing parent. In fact, it annoys me so much that I'm going to go ahead and do the opposite!" Then most of the time you are likely to go ahead and do exactly that, the opposite of what the "should" or "supposed to" tells you to do. Going back to the example of telling yourself you really should go see your family doctor ASAP, you proceed to do the opposite and not go at all. In turn, this develops into what a real-life lecturing parent ends up with in most instances: a *rebellious kid.* Arguably that's what we all pretty much become when we self-rebel and do the opposite of a "should" message, particularly when that very "should" message is in our best interest to carry out. This reaction by your rebellious kid is what I am referring to as "cognitive split number two."

Let me give you an example of this two-part cognitive split that my client Ira experienced. For the past ten years, Ira has been riding the weight-loss/weight-gain roller coaster. For a few months, Ira would lose the weight. Unfortunately, in the months after that, the pounds came back.

In my previous book *Inner Blocks to Losing Weight*, I talk about how self-rebellion applies on the weight-loss front. Ira's situation epitomizes this. Specifically, for the first few months, Ira typically would have good self-discipline. He almost always ate what he should, no more than he should, and exercised on days when he said he would. All of this positive, self-disciplined behavior on Ira's part certainly was the opposite of self-sabotage, but in a matter of time, Ira's rebellion would inevitably kick in and set a negative momentum in motion. For example, when he would tell himself he *should* only eat artificially sweetened good-ies, Ira would instead eat regular cookies and cake. Then when he would tell himself he *should* "just eat a little bit but not a lot" of his favorite ice cream, Ira would proceed to stuff down a pint or more. When he told himself he *should* exercise after work, he instead typically headed off to a local happy hour instead of the health club.

Putting this all into self-rebellion and two-part-cognitive-split terms, the downhill chain of events for Ira went like this: First, he repeatedly told himself what he should or shouldn't eat and how much he should exercise. In other words, he cognitively split into the "lecturing parent." When he ended up doing exactly the opposite of all of this, he split into a "rebellious kid." By this point, Ira was heading right down the path to regaining his lost weight. His rebellious kid won out again while in the process undermining his internal responsible adult.

In the best of all possible psychological worlds, no one would undergo these issues. Since the chances are that there is no way that's going to happen, the next best thing is to practice switching the "shoulds" into more cooperation-inducing, rebellion-reducing self-commands. Getting back to the example of the "should" about calling your physician, you might want replace the "should" message with something like "Hey you—you have no choice. Call your doctor already!" or "Come on, time to call the doctor once and for all!" Statements like these take you out of the cognitive mode of both the lecturing parent and the rebellious kid. Instead, you simply become the *responsible adult*, one who does not lecture nor behaves like a typical rebellious kid. This responsible adult chooses only to do what's in your best interest, utilizing the tools of self-control and self-discipline. Additionally, a responsible adult generally does quite well keeping your daily assortment of "shoulds" and "supposed to's" to a minimum.

Self-Rebellion, "Shoulds," Your Inner Bully, and Agitation

It's time now to bring the inner bully back into the mix. The villain behind all of your automatic, frequent "shoulds" that gets your two-part cognitive split going is your favorite nemesis, your inner bully. In turn, this gets your self-rebellious, oppositional behavior going and pushes more of your self-Respect out the window. Once again, the vicious circle of should-induced self-sabotaging can continue on and on, likely over quite extended periods of time.

Think of your inner bully as, amongst other things, a master of both understanding and manipulating behavior. Unfortunately though, this master is also like a proverbial "mad scientist," conjuring up ways to use the information it gathers to attempt to wreak havoc on people like you.

Imagine if you will that many lifetimes ago, one of the earliest inner bullies figured out that most human beings, especially those with dysfunctional upbringings, are easy prey for addictively self-rebellious behavior. More specifically, one might conjecture that this "ancestral" inner bully brilliantly yet deviously concluded that it can have a rip-roaringly sabotaging effect on people. You could say that this behavior was then passed on through many "generations" of inner bullies, right up to the present generation.

Let's return to Jennifer again. Jennifer actually was a highly intelligent and talented woman, who had a great sense of humor, was compassionate and helpful, and gave helpful advice to others. Alas, in spite of these appealing qualities, poor Jennifer remained at the mercy of her addictive use of "shoulds" and her resultant job-related and relationship-related episodes of self-sabotage. Therefore, the only advice Jennifer ended up taking in these situations was the very bad advice she kept getting from her inner bully, that is, to self-rebel!

What does this whole ongoing pattern of "shoulding on" yourself, two-part cognitive splitting, self-rebellion, and self-sabotaging ultimately add up to? It can leave you with a whole lot of churning inside. As you know by now, this agitation gives your inner bully a virtually never-ending supply of psychological ammunition to use against you, ammunition which as underscored before can used by your inner bully to keep addicted to self-sabotaging self-rebellion, and in the end low self-Worth.

In case it isn't obvious, you can view *all* addictive behavior as self-rebellion. Whether we are talking about overeating, excessive drinking, drug use, or pathological gambling, every addictive act involves doing the opposite of what's in your best interest. Hence, every addictive act you perform is an act of compulsive self-rebellion. In turn, this does exactly what your inner bully loves by keeping your core self-Worth below where you want and need it to be.

To recap, self-rebellion is doing the opposite of what is in your best interest. This self-rebellion can be thought of as addictive if it is a pattern of behavior that is in control of you and causes you some type of harm, whether it's psychological, physical, financial, or relationship-related. Self-rebellion is triggered in part by the excessive use of self-commanding "shoulds." These create a two-part cognitive split into "lecturing parent" mode followed immediately into "rebellious kid" mode. Self-rebellion heightens core agitation, which is used by the inner bully as one more type of ammunition in its arsenal to create the potential for self-sabotage.

Exercise

In what situations more than any others do you tell yourself that you are "supposed to" or "should" do something?

In what situations, if any, do you usually refuse to give in to the "rebellious kid" even when you have been bombarded by the "lecturing parent"?

Make a list of words or phrases that you believe will help you cut down on your use of "shoulds" to replace your "two-part cognitive split" with pure, responsible adult self-motivation.

Chapter 6

Outer Bullies

"BULLIES ARE ALWAYS COWARDS AT HEART, and may be 'credited' with a dead-on instinct for scenting their prey." —Anna Julia Cooper

"Bullying is like fire: it can burn you emotionally and physically; at the same time, the smoke it leaves in your soul can choke away your courage too."—Benjamin Disraeli (paraphrased)

Within the past decade, the subject of bullying has become a topic of a great deal of scrutiny among academicians, researchers, school personnel, parents, and documentary filmmakers. The prevalence of bullying in schools and the workplace has led to measures to crack down on it, often under the heading of "zero tolerance." Bullying, of course, is nothing new. It's safe to assume that it has been occurring earlier than the Stone Age when Neanderthals reigned supreme.

Over the many millennia that have passed since then, it appears very unfortunately that more modern "Neanderthals" or bullies have managed to escape extinction and continue to menace the world around them. These real-life antagonists can be considered *outer* bullies, to distinguish them from their cronies, the *inner* bullies.

Bullying: Definitions and Psychological Effects

In his "Bullying Prevention Program," Dan Oliveus offered this definition of bullying: "A person is bullied when he/she is exposed repeatedly to negative actions on the part of one or more persons, as a result of which he/she ends up having a great deal of difficulty defending themselves." Oliveus implies that bullying essentially triggers a feeling of "learned helplessness," a phrase coined by psychologist Martin Seligman in the mid-1970s.

On a Web site entitled "Life After Adult Bullying," Carolyn Laithwaite addresses some prototypical characteristics common to most outer bullies. These include low self-Worth, seething resentment if not bitterness, jealousy, feelings of inadequacy, masked shame, and strong prejudices. Laithwaite also underscores the commonly seen, strong likelihood that outer bullies were in some way bullied themselves as children.

Another possible definition for bullying can be found online in Wikipedia, where it is defined as "the use of force or coercion to abuse or intimidate others. The behavior can be habitual, and involve an imbalance of social and/or physical power. It can include verbal harassment or threat, physical assault, or verbal coercion, and may be directed toward particular victims, perhaps on grounds of race, religion, gender, sexuality, or ability."

Regardless of the author or academician presenting a definition or perspective on bullying, it's safe to say that outer bullies can "sniff out" your vulnerabilities and pounce on them. It could be your physical appearance, intelligence, social discomfort, "weird" name, or whatever it is that predators like these consider as fair game for their mean-spirited, bullying "jollies."

"Direct hitters" Versus "Sneak attackers"

There are two categories of outer bullies, which correspond to the two self-sabotaging ways that your *inner* bully gets you: "direct hitters" and "sneak attackers." To review from back in Chapter 2, direct hitters are outer bullies who hit hard verbally and/or physically. From verbally attacking statements like "You are truly ugly!" to "You will never get anywhere in life!" these verbal direct hits can hurt you in your "psychological solar plexus." Then there are the *physical* direct hitters, the outer bullies who are the literal hitters, pushers, slappers, or punchers. These are the "pseudo-machos" of the world, acting real tough when at the core they are just emotional weaklings somewhat like sheep in wolves' clothing rather than the standard vice versa. Unfortunately, however, the hurt to the *actual* solar plexus that physical outer bullies cause is of course not "pseudo" hurt but the real thing!

However, I want to focus more on the category of sneak attackers. Unlike the direct-hitting outer bullies, sneak attackers do not consciously hurt whoever is on the receiving end of their bullying. Nonetheless, sneak-attacking outer bullies can in certain ways hurt you in your emotional core even more than direct hitters can. Keep in mind too that unlike direct hitters whose verbal and physical bullying is easily observable, sneak attackers tend to be more *in*direct and therefore not as clear-cut and obvious a type of bullying as direct hitting.

More specifically, think of these sneak attackers as falling into three possible categories: neglectors, abandoners, and what will be called "schizophrenogenics."

Neglectful outer bullies are, as previously noted, any parent or significant other who hurts you via frequent and significant neglect on the affection front, or fails to spend time with you. Neglector outer bullies tend to be overcritical, underpraising, work an excessive number of hours on the job, withdraw into their own world a lot, and/or spend a disproportionate amount of time socializing with others outside the home.

Perhaps the one way a neglector outer bully may try to meet your needs is on the *material* front, by often buying you things that you genuinely enjoy. The reality here, however, is that for most people who feel neglected, material giving can never replace or compensate for insufficient giving on the affection and time fronts. The feeling of deprivation that you experience basically has another aspect to it. Specifically, feeling neglected is based every bit as much on the absence of any sincere, consistent, and ongoing attempts on the neglector bully's part to try to *make it up* to you. It is one thing if a parent or partner of yours works a lot, stays out often, or withdraws into themselves frequently. It is another when that same neglecting outer bully does not try with any consistency to make it up to you especially by spending more time with you or being more attentive. It is this second piece of the puzzle that creates a double whammy, which can leave you feeling unlovable at the core.

Abandoning types of outer bullies are, as noted previously, potentially even more psychologically damaging to the person on the receiving end of this abandonment than neglecting outer bullies. Abandoning outer bullies do not simply neglect you at various times. They outright abandon you. In my experience, the basis for the act of abandoning tends to be either *spite*— for example, toward the child's other biological parent—and/ or simply a cowardly, inexcusable abandonment of *parental duties* due to feeling overwhelmed by their responsibilities. From my perspective, there is little room for compassion in the latter case, since the motive for the abandonment is basically a combination of being self-serving plus succumbing to weak-willed panic. In contrast, there is very little room for compassion when the excuse is spite, because ongoing spite basically reflects the absence of a conscience. After all, can it take anything *but* a lack of conscience to essentially throw an innocent child or children to the wolves?

Schizphrenogenic outer bullies are in a separate category of sneak-attackers. Schizophrenogenic outer bullies typically do not in any obvious way attack, neglect, or outright abandon their children. Instead, they bully in ways that are subtler than the sneak-attacking neglector and abandoning outer bullies. This type of outer bully essentially plays the role of a mixed-messaging *martyr*.

The labeling of someone as being a "schizophrenogenic" is in my experience a very underdiscussed and fascinating label, one that warrants putting it under a microscope to truly grasp the complexity of the behavior. The term was first coined in 1956 by the brilliant communication-oriented research team of Gregory Bateson, Don Jackson, John Weakland, and Jay Haley. As this fearless foursome underscored, labeling someone as schizophrenogenic is not equivalent to being labeled a schizo-*phrenic*. A schizophrenic is, sadly enough, a deeply pained soul. He/she is someone who for the most part cannot function in life without the right regimen. If however that person maintains that medication regimen, the chances are they will be able to function adequately if not effectively in some important areas of their lives, be it in school, on the job, and in significant relationships. In the process, schizophrenics can end up having their self-distressing, psychologically debilitating symptoms (for example, hearing voices and paranoid thinking) kept in check.

As for schizophrenogenics, there is no (and I only use this word in a stereotypic, totally non-judgmenal way) "crazy" behavior or thinking exhibited. Instead, schizophrenogenics can be thought of as driving *other* people crazy! To clarify, you can assume that someone subjected to ongoing schizophrenogenic communication may never end up becoming a full-blown schizophrenic himself (as was the perspective originally explored by Bateson et al.). Clinically speaking, however, they still might end up suffering from symptoms of, e.g., depression, anxiety, panic attacks, and/or substance abuse.

The essence of a schizophrenogenic is in their pattern of an ongoing and unintended accumulation of psychologically "discombobulating" communications. People on the receiving end of this psychologically communicational pattern can end up feeling bombarded with four basic mixed messages: "Do as I say, not as I do!" "You never are good enough for me!" "Why can't you be like your (sibling/cousin/friend)?" "You don't really love me, even though you say you do!" Unnerving statements like these can boil down to can't-win, guilt-tripping, negatively-comparing, "damned if you do/don't" communications. These messages imply the required and relentless pursuit of perfection, which the Bateson team called "double-bind" communications (an excellent summary of their work is provided in a 2006 article in a journal called Psychotherapy In Australia, entitled "Still Crazy-Making after All These Years," by psychologist Paul Gibney).

Allow me to present an example of a double-binding dialogue, between Rochelle and her schizophrenogenic mother:

Mother: "Rochelle, now tell me the truth. Did you remember that tomorrow is my birthday?"

Rochelle: "Oh my God, Mom. You know that I've been so caught up for weeks now in (husband) Barry's job situation. You know how nervous I've been about that really bad cough that (son) Adam still has, so I must confess, I totally forgot. I'm sorry!"

Mother (in a distinctly pouty voice): "Well, Rochelle, you know I understand that Barry and Adam have to come first in your life."

Rochelle (tenseness rising in her almost plea-like voice): "You know, Mom, I really hope you do understand, Mom. I really do!"

Mother: "I do, honey, but to tell you the truth, it's times like this that I end up wondering if you really even love your mother anymore or need her in your life."

Rochelle: "Oh, Mom, of course I do! Please, you do know that, right?"

Mother: "Yes I do, dear, but I feel like you hardly ever make time for me anymore especially since your father died last year."

Rochelle (with some positive-sounding energy returning in her voice): "OK, Mom, tell you what. On Saturday, let's go to that new lunch restaurant that everyone is raving about so we can celebrate your birthday and then do some shopping!"

Mother: "See, now you're just saying that because I told you that you never give me any time. I think you now feel obligated to ask me out for my birthday. Am I right?"

Rochelle (in tears): "Oh for God's sake, Mom. I just really can't win with you, can I? If I apologize and offer to take you out for your birthday, you don't think I'm being sincere. On the other hand, if I forget your birthday and don't apologize, then you think I'm showing you I don't love or need you. Either way, I just can't win with you, and that really drives me crazy!"

Mother: "Now dear, why are you getting so defensive?"

Given this type of double-binding dialogue between Rochelle and her schizophrenogenic mother, is it any coincidence that generally well-liked Rochelle suffers from clinical symptoms of anxiety and depression? Yes, there may be other significant stresses in Rochelle's life unrelated to her mother. Nonetheless, it's hard to imagine that except maybe for the most thick-skinned, mentally healthy of souls, who *wouldn't* end up clinically affected by this ongoing pattern of double-binding communication, much less from someone as important to you as one of your parents or your significant other?

Because of this virtually inevitable development and persistence of psychological problems in the recipient of double-binding communications, I choose to label schizophrenogenics as a category of outer bullies. Still, as with the other types of outer bullies, I cannot emphasize enough that schizophrenogenics can at the same time be genuinely loving and caring people as well! The problem is that this message all too often gets lost in the double-binding translation.

Outer Bullies and Your Inner Bully

You may recall that the inner bully is essentially an inner "echo." The echo is all the direct-hitting and sneak-attacking communications coming from mostly loving, well-meaning parents and significant others in your growing years. As underscored previously, these two disturbing categories of communication and the related echo created inside you accumulate over the years to become the voice of your inner bully.

Viewed from this perspective, I hope it makes sense to you that your inner bully basically feeds off of any and all outer bullies in your life, current or past. Therefore, the more you have been bullied in some way shape or form by any outer bullies, the more you can assume that your *inner* bully has taken all of those bullying communications and absorbed them like a sponge. Then it's pretty much "ventriloquist" time for your inner bully, armed as it now is with plenty of ammunition to self-sabotagingly use against you. In the process, it makes you believe you are—to once again sum it up—"never (doing) good enough." Which, as you know by now, will in turn likely be reflected in ending up with low self-Worth at best, and clinical symptoms like depression and/or anxiety and/or substance abuse or other addictive behaviors at worst.

Overall then, the goal for anyone and everyone in dealing with outer bullies is to do your best to stand up to these psychologically distressing individuals, once and for all. In most instances, that's a lot easier said than done as you can I'm sure imagine, the process often requiring a great deal of courage on your part to do so. No matter what though, whether dealing with verbal or physical bullying, asserting yourself with an outer bully is best done by letting him/her know in no uncertain terms that their ways of communicating to you are totally unacceptable! Of course, asserting yourself this way does not guarantee that the person will end up backing off from you, much less backing away entirely. What *is* guaranteed is the gain you will experience in your core self-Respect—and therefore in turn in your core self-Worth. That gain will be true even if the particular outer bully of focus does not really back down much in the end anyway.

One more thought on bullying before wrapping up this chapter. If you think about it, bullying is by no means limited to one-on-one or few-on-one contexts. History gives unending evidence of much larger-scale bullying, that is, cultural bullying, religious bullying, and nationalistic bullying—that is, bullying ad nauseam. In fact you might just characterize these types of bullying as, sadly enough, indicative of widespread *in*human— rather than human—nature.

On that note, it's time now to shift focus off of how your inner bully keeps you down and on to ways to learn how to stand up to it and put it in its place. Coming up in the final three chapters are sets of strategies to help you accomplish that. One set of strategies (Chapter 7) are *individual*, inner bully–challenging strategies you can use on your own with no one else having to be involved. These are primarily for the purpose of helping you manage your core agitation better and build up your core self-Worth separate from the important relationships in your life.

The second set of strategies (Chapter 8) to be presented are *relationship*-related strategies. These especially involve strategies you can practice for making your important relationships healthier ones *or* for eventually extricating yourself quicker than you usually do from the unhealthy ones. Either direction will certainly require sustained courage on your part, yet neither guarantees anything at all about outer bullies in your life backing down from you. Nonetheless, all of these strategies can in turn add up to—once again—gains in your core self-Worth, no matter where your efforts take you. In the process, you can end up cutting down on the number of situations in your life in which your inner bully—on both the self-sabotage and the relationship-sabotage fronts—typically wins, while you therefore typically lose. To put this in a Biblical way, the strategies presented in the final two chapters of the book can help you bring out your "inner David" to stand up to your "inner Goliath"!

Last but not least, the final set of strategies discussed (Chapter 9) are strategies for preventing self-sabotage in the *workplace*.

Before moving on, here's another exercise.

Exercise

1. Think back over the years of your life and identify the individuals who you feel bullied you. For each of these individuals listed, identify which category (if not catego-r*ies*) of outer bully each individual bully fits into.

2. For each outer bully listed, specify how you attempted to cope with the bullying; for example, you basically did nothing, tried ignoring and/or retreating but usually neither worked, or tried asserting yourself and it at least sometimes worked, which may have gotten the particular outer bully in your life to make some changes in how they treated you, temporarily if not indefinitely.

3. Overall, how would you sum up what you feel has been the cumulative psychological/emotional effect that the ongoing bullying you were subjected to has had on you to this day?

PART TWO

Chapter 7

Standing Up to Your Self-Sabotaging Inner Bully—Individual Strategies

"Self-worth...is learned. And the family is where it is learned...Feelings of worth can only flourish in an atmosphere where individual differences are appreciated, mistakes are tolerated, communication is open, and rules are flexible—the kind of atmosphere that is found in a nurturing family...Since the feeling of worth has been learned, it can be *un*learned, and something new can be learned in its place. The possibility for this learning lasts from birth to death, so it is never too late. There is always hope that your life can change because you can always learn new things."—Virginia Satir

"Facing it—always facing it—that's the *courageous* way to get through."—Joseph Conrad (italics added)

As you know by now, most people who are subjected to some type of bullying over the years end up with one tough *inner* bully to fight. The inner bully then becomes the driving force behind the ways you sabotage yourself in various contexts of your life, whether it be your lack of self-control over compulsive/addictive tendencies, your actions that can cost you your job, or your behaviors that undermine the special relationships in your life. Fed by the present and past real-life bullies in your life, your inner bully does everything in its power to knock down your core self-Worth.

As presented in Chapter 2, the working definition of courage used in this book is anything you are reluctant or hesitant to do but make yourself do anyway because ultimately it is in your best interest to do that. Whether it's for example telling your boss you deserve a raise after putting off asking for months now, telling a close friend who often gets right on the defensive that they have been doing things that hurt the friendship you have with them, or starting a small business you have been wanting to start for a long time, these are some self-respecting ways to make that courage come to life. Courage is one of your best allies in life, while being an "enemy" of your inner bully at the same time.

A "Menu" of Courageous Strategies for Standing Up to Your Inner Bully

Let me offer you now a "menu" of self-help strategies to mindfully use to get your core self-Worth up to a level you want it to be. As with a real menu, you are welcome to choose the same item or items each time you use the menu or you can select different items if you want to try something new.

There are seven basic, self-empowering items on this menu: exercises for building up self-Esteem and self-Respect, agitation management, guilt management, more consistent self-discipline, more consistent pursuit of pleasure/relaxation, clarifying your sense of purpose in your life, and professional help.

Building Up Core Self-Worth

Back in Chapter 2, a two-pronged approach to building up more overall self-Worth was presented. As a quick recap, on the self-Esteem front, creating a a self-esteem list allows you to gain clarity on what you like about yourself on the inside rather than the outside. On the self-Respect front, the use of your Self-Credit Time list can help remind you daily of all the "little" things you are accomplishing in your life. While at the time you do them they may only feel like little accomplishments, over time they can add up to reaching the big goals you set for work, school, parenting, romance, or domestic tasks. Keep in mind too that when you come right down to it, self-Respect as part of the self-Worth equation counts more than self-Esteem.

Agitation Management

As emphasized in Chapter 4, all of the churning you may have going on inside leaves your inner bully with some psychologically powerful ammunition to use against you. The more agitation the bully creates, the more likely you will get trapped in tunnel focus. On the other hand, the more manageable your agitation becomes, the more you will be able to think clearly, maintain good short-term memory, cultivate an appropriate range of emotions, exhibit good judgment, and, best of all, have fun. Getting your agitation down and keeping it manageable is really just what the doctor ordered for putting your inner bully in its place and enjoying your life more in the process!

There are four strategies I especially recommend for keeping your agitation level manageable at minimum, and generally low at maximum. At this level, you have a fighting chance to slowly but surely shift your tendency to be very self-critical into becoming more self-reinforcing and self-crediting—much to your inner bully's dismay. These strategies are: emotional venting, diversions, meditation, "get physical," and guilt management.

Emotional Venting

By venting any overpowering negative emotion, you begin to empower yourself to prevent your inner bully from steering you into some self-sabotaging direction.. This venting can be done by journaling, sharing your feelings with someone you know trust, or getting physical in some energetic way.

Journal venting basically involves getting some type of writing device like a spiral notebook or your computer, and using it to "let it all out" emotionally through the written word. It especially can be helpful if you give yourself carte blanche to, if you so choose, disregard grammar and spelling, write in large letters with lots of exclamation points, and allow yourself to sprinkle some "choice" words into the mix whenever needed.

Journal entries like these do not have to be done daily; they can be done purely on an as-needed basis. Entries can be made in an open-ended, unstructured manner or with some structure, for example, in the form of a letter. It does not matter whether you write two sentences, two paragraphs, or two pages. All that matters is that you bring up the emotion into consciousness and then let it out .

Vocal venting has two possibilities. The first is the easier of the two. It's sharing your emotions directly with a trusted friend or family member. However, you want to be careful about the *timing* of your sharing as well as the person's willingness to listen. The second of the two choices is "symbolic confrontation." This agitation-management tool is not for everyone by any means. But assuming you are willing to give it a try, I recommend you make it an option especially for *anger* management more than anything else.

A symbolic confrontation requires you to go somewhere where you are guaranteed privacy with assurance that no one will hear you when you speak out loud. This could especially be either in your residence if no one is home and you have sound-proof walls, or in your car. If you choose the latter, you get into your car and either keep it parked, or drive a short distance to a parking lot that has an isolated portion. Then wherever you are at the moment, picture that the person who is the object of your anger is sitting next to you. You then proceed to let loose—although what I mean here by "letting loose" is to be *blunt*. For example, suppose you are resentful of your boss' tendency to talk belittilingly to you, but you don't want to run the risk of what you believe are likely negative consequences if you tell him/her directly about your resentment. What you can do about your justifiable anger is have a symbolic confrontation, in which you picture your boss sitting there next to you as vividly as possible. You then proceed to bluntly confront him/her loudly with statements along the lines of "Look, I've got something to get off my chest, and you are going to sit here and listen to me whether you want to or not!" From there, you persist in remaining in blunt mode, spelling out your specific resentments. You continue your bluntness until you feel you've gone as far as you can and stop there. By doing this type of symbolic confrontation, you decrease the odds that you would ever actually give in to the impulse to verbally explode at your boss directly. In the process, you give yourself the needed opportunity to let off some agitation-based "steam," in a vigorous and highly charged manner. By doing this, you cannot emotionally hurt anyone nor will you receive any significant negative consequences for being out of line. In other words, you get the opportunity to "hit and run" in a safe way that allows the intensity of your agitation to become more manageable without any consequences to you *or* to the other person.

The third type of venting is *getting physical*. It can be some form of exercise, playing the drums, cleaning the house, or gardening. Whichever activity you choose, the chances are you know from experience that getting physical in some way, shape, or form can be an effective tool to lower your level of being all churned up inside.

Diversions

Diversions are a second way to get your agitation level down to a manageable level. The choice of diversion you make goes under the heading of "different strokes for different folks." For example, one person's diversion may be listening to music or reading, another person may prefer running or playing tennis, and a third person can enjoy gardening or cooking. All that matters is that you pursue whichever diversions bring your agitation level down and your enjoyment of your life up!

Meditation and "Abridged" Meditation

Last but not least is the practice of meditation. Whether it takes the form of specific breathing techniques, guided imagery, yoga, or some type of prayer, any one of these or combination thereof can create a relaxing, peaceful, agitation-reduced state of being. On a personal note on the guided imagery front, one of my favorite little visual images is a snarling pit bull attacking your inner bully. In this case, you end up with a battle between your (pardon another pun) inner pit bull vs. your inner bully! You might also try using an *auditory* image, such as imagining you can hear someone you respect telling you to "Take control!" or "Hey, that's just your inner bully trying to mess with you!"

Some of you may have difficulty with meditative techniques, particularly if you have symptoms of Obsessive-Compulsive Or Attention Deficit Disorder. If you are challenged by one or both of these psychological conditions, meditation probably is going to be more difficult for you to practice, and you may find that the other agitation-management menu items work better for you. That's not to say that there are *never* times when individuals with those disorders can end up feeling some degree of peace via the use of meditation. However, people with OCD or ADHD tend to have a greater vulnerability to tunnel focus and heightened agitation due to their obsessive nature and difficulty paying attention. These traits make it much more difficult to shut out the rest of the world or use soothing imagery of some type, be it by the ocean, in the woods, or in some spiritual sanctuary. All is not lost, though, because it is possible to practice something I like to call "abridged" meditation. The key to this approach is in the use of a self-chosen *mantra*.

For anyone not familiar with that term, think of a mantra as a shorthand way of breaking through tunnel focus and reducing internal churning. A mantra can be one word or phrase, but preferably no longer than a few words. There will be some trial and error involved in coming up with the mantra that works best for you. Possible mantras include "calm down," "you can do it," be in the moment," or "God give me courage." My personal favorite is the word *dignity*. I think of dignity as the capacity to maintain composure and emotional self-control when feeling attacked in some way. More on the mantra of dignity later.

Once you have chosen your mantra, you need to practice mindfully going to it when you find yourself in a state of heightened agitation. You can pair the mantra with slow deep breathing or with self-soothing imagery. Or you can also keep repeating (essentially chanting) the chosen mantra over and over for as long as you want to, as slowly or rapidly as you want. Should you choose the rapid route, you try to match the speed of your chanting with the speed of your racing thoughts, which gives you the potential control to slow them down. You can even add an unobtrusive physical component, like rubbing your fingers or, believe it or not, something my lovable but a bit eccentric friend Sue recommended: chattering your teeth (with your mouth closed of course). You should always remember that some trial and error may very well be involved in your choice of mantra. One mantra that works for a while may not provide the same benefit after a few weeks. In that case, you simply switch around your mantra until your updated choice does what you need it to do. This process is similar to adjusting your medication until you find the one at the right dose at the appropriate time of day.

In sum, the moral of the story on the use of meditation is this: if by nature you tend to be a "compartmentalizer," then chances are you will do well with ongoing practice of some type of meditation. On the other hand, if you tend to be easily distracted or obsessively focused, then I recommend not putting too many of your agitation-management "eggs" into a traditional meditation "basket." Remember, you still have several other strategies described above: situational abridged meditation, emotional/physical venting, and the pursuit of diversions.

Oh, and one more thing about meditation. As a massage therapist colleague and friend of mine Amy Garmon once pointed out to me, for some people, meditation is not very helpful while in a stationary position lying down or sitting. That would especially apply to people with ADHD or a general "hyperness," people who can't sit still for very long–people like *me* frankly! Instead, as Amy empahatically underscored to me, people like us are candidates for forms of "*moving*" meditation. That's right, moving meditation—such as doing some form of exercise, or gardening, or engaging in a physical type of hobby. After all, the goal of meditation is to achieve a more peaceful relaxed state, right? Well, for many people that can occur in a stationary postion of some type. But for others like yours truly, yes, we can sometimes be stationary meditators for sure. But at enough other times we get more relaxed and less agitated when on the move, doing something enjoyable and productive. For those of you folks who prefer the stationary types of meditation though, well, they don't call it different strokes for different folks for nothing, right?

Get Physical!

This one is pretty basic—and can be pretty darn useful for getting your agitation down to a manageable level. Options here especially include exercise, gardening, house cleaning, or anything else that gets you physically siphoning off excessive agitation. Your choice here—and your choice here as to when and how often you go any one or more of these routes.

Guilt Management

As you have already learned, your inner bully knows how to use the several different components of your core agitation as fuel for sabotage against you. One of the most significant of these components that your inner bully taps into so to speak is major, unresolved, typically irrational *guilt*. It could be guilt over something recent, from decades ago, or anything in between. All that matters is that the guilt is intense enough to distress you. Unlike some of the other components of agitation such as bitterness, betrayal, and jealousy though, guilt is often acknowledged openly and directly.

You basically have three options for reducing your guilt down to a manageable level. The first option is some religiously prescribed form of confession. I am mainly referring to a ritualistic form of atonement prescribed by your choice of organized religion. For example, if you are a practicing Catholic, you can repent by going to confession. If you are a Jewish, you can do your penance by fasting and attending service on Yom Kippur. The bottom line here is if you see yourself as religious in some way, then chances are you will experience at least some reduction in your agitation-based guilt if you engage in a religiously prescribed form of contrition. However, in order to truly benefit psychologically from these religiously prescribed acts of attrition, the chances are you must truly feel a deep commitment to your chosen religion and God. Otherwise, based on many of the experiences shared with me by nonpracticing people, you are not likely to experience much guilt reduction if you are just going through the motions. Luckily, there are other options to reduce guilt.

I have labeled the second guilt-reducing technique as *personal penance*. Personal penance is not an act of self-cleansing prescribed by a church or clergyman. Personal penance is really about *making amends*. For example, suppose you feel guilty after hurting someone important to you. If you decide you want to go this route, there are two types of ways to do a personal penance. The first and more obvious of the two involves offering a sincere, heartfelt apology to the person you hurt. Preferably this would be done face-to-face or at least over the phone. Apologizing with the tools of modern technology is strongly discouraged. Sincerity must reign supreme here or else your apology will go over like a lead balloon.

The second strategy for personal penance involves making reparations, i.e., amends, to help the other person in some genuinely useful way. Examples include domestic assistance, financial aid, or spending some enjoyable social time together. This is something you can pursue at one time only or over a reasonable period of days, weeks, or months if indicated. You may recognize that the most healing type of atonement you can do is the one that the emotionally injured person truly *appreciates*. Therefore, you don't for example try to make amends by getting someone who is not a sports fan a free ticket to a football game or by purchasing roses for a woman who had an ex-husband who typically gave her flowers after his indiscretions. In other words, you really need to give some thought as to what your specific choice of amend-making will be for this specific person.

It is possible some of you may be asking, "What if the person I have harmed is already deceased? How could I make restitution then?" Let's suppose you feel guilty because you believe you did not spend enough time with the deceased person before he/she passed or you feel angry with yourself for not saying good-bye. Keep in mind that in these situations, it typically does not matter if virtually everyone else believes that you did spend a *great deal* of time attending to this loved one in numerous ways. All that matters here is that *you* feel you didn't do enough or give enough to that loved one regardless of anyone else's opinion on the matter. Despite the fact that on some level you may recognize that this irrational compulsion for confession is related to your inner bully's machinations, you may still want to utilize one or both of the techniques created for these circumstances.

The more "direct" type of posthumous amend-making involves composing a heartfelt, detailed letter of apology to your loved one. Whenever you feel that you are ready, bring this letter to your loved one's gravesite. At the burial site, look at the gravestone or the sky and recite your letter of apology out loud. You do this with the faith that your loved one's spirit can clearly hear your heartfelt words. Expect though, as you can probably imagine, that this will be an intensely emotional experience to go through!

A second, more indirect "posthumous" amend-making is to make yourself do something that you can think of as a *symbolic* gesture of penance. For example, your choice of personal atonement could be to perform volunteer work in a nursing home if your loved one was elderly or in the children's unit of a hospital if the loved one was young.

Personal penance is best used by those who do not see themselves as truly religious, but it can also work well for those who see themselves as spiritual. It may even be beneficial to the religiously minded if they use it in conjunction with more traditional forms of absolution.

The third strategy I recommend for guilt reduction involves a process I call *permission work*. This process starts with the assumption that one of the basic self-sabotaging messages you have been receiving all your life from your inner bully is, in so many words, "You are not allowed to forgive yourself for anything bad that you did!"

"Permission work" is a strategy to gradually convince yourself that you *are* allowed to forgive yourself once and for all. Even more importantly, permission work can help you psychologically heal from the guilt caused by any major, self-defined transgression you committed. The key here is to recognize that your inner bully will not give you the permission to forgive yourself. Therefore, in order to gradually reduce your guilt's intensity, you will need permission to make that happen. This requires the permission of someone *outside* of you. This is what I call the permission-giving process.

The permission-giving process is essentially a reconditioning process. The goal of the permission-giving process is to gradually recondition your core negative belief that you are not allowed forgiveness into an exact opposite set of beliefs. Through this reconditioning, you can end up believing that you *are* allowed, have permission, and deserve to forgive yourself and heal from your self-defined transgression(s). The reconditioning can also be useful in regard to challenging those negative beliefs you may have about yourself related to others' past judgments.

The permission-giving process involves electing someone in your life to fill the important role of *permission-giver*. The person you elect to this role must meet the following three stringent criteria:

1) The person is a straight shooter. He/she tells it like it is in a direct but nonattacking, nonjudgmental manner. You also know too that the person sincerely cares about you.

2) The person has *true empathy* for anything that causes you emotional pain. For example, that person suffers from anxiety, panic attacks, addiction, or depression just like you do so when that person tells you he/she understands what you are going through, he/she really does understand your plight as opposed to someone coming along and saying, "Oh, I know what you mean," when you know for a fact that despite being well-intentioned, that person can't possibly know exactly what you are going through simply because the person hasn't experienced it.

3) You trust in this person and respect him/her based on how he/she lives his/her life and how he/she treats you.

In my experience, most people completing this exercise are able to identify someone in their personal lives who meets all three criteria. That person could be a significant romantic other, a parent, a friend, an adult child, a boss, or a clergyman.

Unfortunately, there are people who cannot identify anyone in their lives who meet all three criteria. In that case, you have the option of choosing the person in your life who you feel best fits the bill. Once you have chosen your permission-giver, the chances are very strong that this person will gladly accept the role and be flattered that you chose him/her. Sometimes, a person chooses the therapist as the permission-giver, which in my experience typically works out fine as an option.

At that point, you and your permission-giver will conduct what I call reconditioning permission-giving "mini-sessions." These mini-sessions should not last more than two minutes maximum per session and should be done three times per week. The total expenditure of time across all three sessions generally amounts to five to six minutes. In addition, the mini-sessions do not require face-to-face contact. They can be done over the phone but preferably not by e-mail or texting since hearing the permission giver's voice is important here.

The permission-giving sessions proceed as follows: As the permission seeker, you will go first. The format you will follow should be something like "I still feel as though I'm not allowed to _____." You fill in the blank with the specific transgression you committed and, if relevant, who you "sinned" against. For example, your statement might be "I still feel as though I'm not allowed to *forgive myself for neglecting my father before he died!*" In a different context, suppose deep down you believe others' negative judgments about you count more than your own positive opinions about yourself. Your statement might then be "I still feel as though I'm not allowed to *make my own positive opinions about myself count more than my parents!*" Suppose deep down you believe you are not allowed to see yourself as a good person who deserves to be happy in life. Your statement here would be "I still feel as though I'm not allowed to *believe I'm a good person who deserves to be happy in life!*"

Once your permission-seeking statement is expressed, your role in the process is completed. Now it's your permsiion-giver's turn. The response that he/she will make is the following reflective, nonjudgmental statement: "By the power you have vested in me as your permission-giver, I give you full permission to begin right now and from here on in to _____!" Your permission-giver then fills in the blank with your self-defined transgression such as any of the three presented above. At that point the mini-session is completed. With practice, it is likely to take less than a minute to complete.

What should you expect to feel at the end of each mini-session? You should begin to develop a quiet foundational feeling that basically involves planting a seed of knowledge that you are making progress in your ability to stand up to your inner bully and say (in so many words), "I'm *done* with all of this guilt, and it's time to start really seeing good things about myself!" The more mini-sessions you do with your permission-giver, the quicker you will reach the point of guilt resolution. Figure this process will take a while though to really hit home.. Ultimately, the goal of the permission-giving process is to reach a point where you no longer *need* a permission-giver! When you get to this level of achievement, you will know for sure that your inner bully's power over you will drastically decline.

However, you might want to keep in mind that in its never-ending resourceful way, your inner bully is quite capable of sabotaging this permission-giving process. How? By convincing you that deep down, you do not have its permission to *believe* the permission you are getting from your permission-giver! With that unfortunate yet realistic possibility in mind, here's the way to circumvent it. Given some credibility I am hoping I have gained in your eyes by this point, I ask you to allow *me* to be your "expert consultant" permission-giver. In that role, I am hereby giving you my full permission to believe that you are allowed to believe *every single word* of forgiveness, positivity, and reassurance that you are seeking from your chosen permission-giver. Knowing that you now have this option for a "backup" permission-giver will likely keep you from feeling you were going to miss the boat on the opportunity for involvement in the permission-giving process.

There are two postscripts I would like to mention on the subject of the permission-giving process. First is something I often see cropping up in my office. Let's suppose you have an important person in your life who has some type of major, self-sabotaging addiction. Also, imagine you are the type of person who irrationally tends to blame *yourself* when you come to see that you cannot "save" or "rescue" someone you love who is messing up his of her life with self-destructive behaviors. To cut down on the self-blame and the resultant guilt your irrational self-blame creates, I highly recommend you get permission from your permission-giver to believe that you are not the cause nor the cure for that other person's addiction. In fact, I recommend you virtually chant these words to yourself like a mantra, that is, "I'm not the cause and I'm not the cure. I'm not the cause and I'm not the cure!"

Postscript number two relates to an important branch of the world of psychotherapy you may or may not be familiar with, called Cognitive Behavior Therapy, or CBT for short. In a nutshell, CBT is used mainly to help people change their self-sabotaging behaviors by changing their self-sabotaging *beliefs* about themselves. Hopefully from what was presented above on permission work, this process is really a prime example of CBT in action Taking that one more step, if you think about it, changing your beliefs about yourself—i.e., self-judgments really—through any and all the ways you stand up to your inner bully really is CBT in action in general.

Self-Discipline and Self-Entertainment Self-discipline and self-entertainment are two more ways to get your self-sabotaging agitation under control and to learn how to stand up to your inner bully. From my perspective, not a whole lot of detail needs to be presented on the subject of self-discipline. Whether it's about maintaining a healthy lifestyle or making progress in other life areas, the path to consistent self-discipline is paved with good intentions. Yet chances are there will be many "potholes" on this path, some of which can cause you to slow down your self-discipline, while others will force you totally off your path. Since your inner bully wants nothing more than for you to sabotage good self-discipline, it is guaranteed to try to keep you vulnerable to detours off the self-discipline path.

The biggest victory your inner bully has on the self-discipline front is when it steers you farther off the path of detours right onto "dead ends." For example, if your goal was to lose weight, then your inner bully would eventually steer you toward self-sabotaging self-rebellion (that is, eating more than you should, eating things you shouldn't, and not exercising when you should). To self-rebel like this for for no more than say two days in a row you should feel free to label as a temporary "detour" and not a dead end. . On the other hand, to self-rebel like this for a few days or more means you have reached a dead end. At this point, it will require you to muster up a lot of energy, determination, and courage on a sustained basis to get back on the self-discipline track. By the same token, your inner bully can get you to lose self-discipline over a wide range of behavioral goals in your life, for example, becoming more organizeed, not relapsing on the substance use front, budgeting your finances, or managing your time better.

You can assume that much to your inner bully's chagrin, the more you maintain consistent self-discipline, the better your overall self-respect. By maintaining enough self-discipline, any slips you make along the way will remain detours and not sink into dead ends.

We have all heard the phrase "everything in moderation." Suppose you emotionally connect self-discipline with self-*deprivation*, a denial from some type of desired pleasure. To get past that type of thinking, you really want to focus on creating some *balance*. Moderation represents the balance between getting *some* pleasure on the one hand via pursuit of some degree of your indulgence of the moment *and* getting some self-Respect for your self-control on the other hand.

Another aspect of your life that your inner bully can sabotage is your pursuit of some preferred type of self-entertainment. More specifically, your inner bully can have you believing at the core that you really don't deserve to entertain yourself in ways that you really enjoy. Yes, occasionally you may get a good laugh in while watching a funny TV show, feel a powerful emotion while reading something you find eye-opening, or feel comforted by a sincere, heartfelt hug. Overall though, your inner bully's attitude toward allowing you some form of self-entertainment essentially boils down to another one of its "forget it Charlie!" declarations.

How do you go about pursuing some form of self-entertainment in spite of your inner bully's attempts to roadblock these pursuits? Two possibilities exist here for shoving your inner bully aside and experiencing some type of self-entertainment, self-relaxation, or some opportunity for self-growth. Possibility number one is to convince yourself you have *earned* the right to pursue some form of self-entertainment. This conviction can be reflected in maintaining good self-discipline and/or reaching some important goal. In other words, you reward yourself for "doing good" in your own eyes.

The second possibility for increasing self-entertainment is to utilize the permission-giving process. Simply put, if you really are blocked and do need it, get permission from your permission-giver to have more pleasure, fun, and entertainment in your life. Hopefully, though, that will be a short-term strategy only until you have your *own* permission to do all this and certainly therefore don't need anyone else's.

Spirituality

If you consider yourself an atheist, I absolutely respect your choice of nonbelief in God or a Higher Power. However, if you are open to hearing some thoughts and musings about God or the Higher Power and/or view yourself as having a strong but nontheist spirituality, then please join me as I venture into this spiritual realm. In this case, spirituality is a means for standing up to your inner bully.

One's personal spiritual belief, which for me equals a nondenominational, nonreligious faith and belief in God, can be significantly affected by the strength of your inner bully. Specifically, I spiritually go under the assumption that the stronger your self-sabotaging inner bully is, the more vulnerable you are to losing faith in God or a Higher Power. Now if you already do not believe in God or a Higher Power and you feel clear and confident about how to lead a spiritually healthy and productive life as an atheist, then I understand that for you there may be no issue here about being negatively influenced by your inner bully. On the other hand, if you are someone who would really like to try to establish or reestablish a connection to God, especially for the sake of having an "ally" inside you for building courage and core self-Worth, then what follows will hopefully fit for you.

From my vantage point, building or rebuilding a connection to God or a Higher Power can be done in either of two ways. One is the traditional way of involvement in an organized religion of your choice. The other is a more personal spiritual direction, for example, joining a nondenominational yet still God-centered spiritual center. Either way you choose, I encourage you to think of this special spiritual ally as always present in your core to assist you in your ongoing battle to keep your inner bully at bay. Whether you pray to God in a traditional way or have a conversation with God in a more personal way, your goal is to come to believe that God is always ready, willing, and able to help you help yourself gain courage and inner strength. Unlike we humans who are prone to being oversensitive in the face of feeling slighted or ignored, if we have not contacted God for a while, my personal belief is that God could not care less if it is days, weeks, months, or even years since we last turned to Him. God understands that you can never know for sure when your inner bully will lead you down the path of your latest act of self-sabotage, right?

As mentioned previously, it is possible that you feel *betrayed* by God. It could be over the death of a loved one, a serious injury that has befallen you or a loved one, dire financial straits, or something evil done to you by a member of the clergy. In the face of any of these potentially faith-shattering situations, I can once again only tell you my own personal belief on the subject, so take this for whatever it's worth to you. In my belief system, God or the Higher Power caused *none* of these life-challenging circumstances, which is a perspective proposed decades ago by Rabbi Harold Kushner in his penetrating book *When Bad Things Happen to Good People.*

Now if you are truly open to a perspective of this nature, then I hope you can eventually come to believe that what God or a Higher Power can do for you is help you cultivate the inner strength and the courage to cope with any major life adversity you may face. In this context, you do not have to think of yourself as "surrendering" to God or a Higher Power. Instead, perhaps you can think of it as seeking God out as your always-availabe, sabotage-controlling, ultimately loving, inner ally.

Professional Help

The last but certainly not least strategy I recommend putting on your "menu" for learning how to stand up to your inner bully is to seek professional help. Simply put, you really ought to consider professional help when your agitation level becomes high enough and persistent enough to manifest in *clinical* problems, like depression, panic attacks, obsessive-compulsive disorder, substance abuse, or many other symptoms. At this stage of the game, your inner bully is pretty much in emotional and psychological control of you, in turn leaving you extra vulnerable to inner bully-triggered acts of self-sabotage and accompaning loss of self-worth. In the worst case scenario, the inner bully steers you down into the abyss of despair, making you more vulnerable to its ultimate terrible victory: suicide—which I propose can also be called "death by inner bully."

When I bring up professional help, there are two options to consider or possibly both of the options together. Option number one is *psychiatric medication.* Enough of you are probably receptive to going the medication route if needed, but enough other people are reluctant at best and unwilling at worst to take medication. However, if you recognize that you really could use some relief from your clinical symptoms, then allow me to propose two analogies to hopefully make it more palatable to you about taking some type of appropriate medication.

Analogy number one is a "vehicle." A vehicle is something you use to get you somewhere you wish to go, but in order for that vehicle to get you there, it needs a driver. When it comes to psychiatric medications, many people in my experience wish or hope that the medication they are prescribed will be both the vehicle *and* the driver. Truth be told, though, you need to view psychiatric medications as the vehicle *only* because like every actual vehicle, this type of vehicle definitely does require a driver. In this case the driver must be you. That means even if you find what you feel is the best vehicle for you, it's still up to you to get into the driver's seat and push yourself to set concrete goals and then take constructive action to reach those goals. Your medication vehicle cannot do the latter for you. If you don't have a vehicle at all, then probably your task is harder. Plus, you should go under the assumption that your inner bully wants you to believe that taking psychiatric medications is nothing but the usual stigmatizing sign of "abnormality" and "weakness" on your part. In the next breath, you want to make sure to remind yourself that those arbitrary judgments are really just—I'll say it again—a bunch of "bull" from your inner bully. If your medications help you manage your core agitation and rebuild your life and core self-Worth, that's a lot more of a statement on courage and self-Respect than "abnormality" or "weakness," don't you think?

Just like a car you might wish to drive, you have the option of "leasing" this vehicle. By doing so, you can either discontinue the use of that vehicle at the end of the lease period or you can choose to keep the vehicle indefinitely. It is the same thing basically with psychiatric meds. Initially, you obligate yourself to "lease" them for the recommended (rather than required) amount of time. When the lease is up, you can either discontinue using the medication or continue using it. In slightly different words, think of taking these types of prescription meds as involving more of a temporary lease than a long-term commitment.

The other analogy I use for taking psychiatric medications is a diabetic's *insulin*. Assuming that your clinical problems are significant and persistent over time and not just situation-induced temporary problems, if you find the right medication for yourself, you might try thinking of it as equivalent to a diabetic staying on insulin. After all, if the right medication keeps your agitation level manageable and therefore keeps you functioning at a comfortable level on a daily basis, as long as there aren't any bad side effects from that medication, you really might as well take *your* insulin everyday too, no?

The other professional option besides medication for helping you stand up to your inner bully is through some form of psychotherapy or counseling. I'm assuming I don't really need to spend much time on this subject. Simply stated, if you know you want or need a therapist or counselor to help you gain a handle on your patterns of self-sabotage and manage your agitation-based clinical problems better, then by all means "seek and ye shall find" one, if possible through a positive personal recommendation. Do yourself a favor and give a trained professional the opportunity to be an external ally in your quest to stand up to your inner bully. After all, we all can use any and every ally we can find in that quest, right?

In review, in this chapter, various strategies were proposed to rein in your inner bully and move forward in your quest for higher self-Worth. The importance of fun diversions, meditation, getting physical, and venting (whether it's in the form of journaling or talking things out with others) was underscored. Also covered were learned ways to manage guilt more appropriately, including making active use of our personal choice of religions or utilizing the permission-giving process. We explored the necessity of developing self-discipline and creating a balance with self-entertainment. Spirituality was reviewed as another tool in our bully-busting toolbox. Lastly, options were discussed for seeking professional help either through psychiatric medication, therapy, or both. Hopefully, some of these weapons will be helpful in waging the battle against your inner bully.

.

Chapter 8

Strategies for Controlling Self-Sabotage in Relationships

"It takes two to tango." —1952 song written by Dick Manning and Al Hoffman

"Love conquers all." —Derived from words of the Greek poet Virgil in approximately AD 80: "Love conquers all things; let us too surrender to love."

An obvious fact of life is that we all need important relationships. Could anyone have put it better than Thomas Merton when he said, "No man (or woman) is an island"? In our personal lives, we can be part of quite a few different relationships, for example, spousal, live-in, serious dating, parent-child, close friend, relative, and neighbor. All of these relationships can be just what the doctor ordered for fulfilling various and sundry needs and desires, from comfort to protection, fun, self-worth, affection, sexual intimacy, and personal growth. Put these all together and you have the creation and maintenance of healthy relationships.

These can be a true godsend in the ultimate pursuit of (personal) life, liberty, and happiness.

That said, let's shift gears back to your inner bully. That antagonist will attempt to steer you into trying to sabotaging any of your relationships in your life. Its number one "weapon of self-Worth destruction" is the core negative belief that you *don't deserve to be happy* in a relationship. When you then go ahead and sabotage important relationships in your life, you leave your inner bully basking in its glory. In turn, this virtually guarantees you will sink into feelings of sadness, loneliness, and/or rejection.

Before I present a list of relationship-sabotaging strategies, go back with me to the two quotes above. Yes, it takes two to tango, literally and figuratively. Now literally speaking, if one dance partner starts doing things that annoy the other partner such as not practicing enough, forgetting certain moves, or getting overcritical, then chances are it's just a matter of time before the annoyed partner parts company on the dance floor (and probably off the floor as well) with the annoying partner. While it takes two to tango, it takes only one to end that tango! This can also apply literally as well in real, non-dance relationships. In these situations, when one member of the relationship decides to end things, you could say that the relationship "tango" is over too.

As for the immortal "love conquers all" notion, from my vantage point, we all grow up conditioned if not brainwashed to believe that this quote speaks the whole truth and nothing but the truth. Well, sorry everyone, but at risk of sounding like a bubble-buster, this romanticized notion is definitely *not* true all of the time by any stretch. In fact, I stand firm in proclaiming that there are two things that love often cannot conquer in a significant relationship: loss of *trust* and loss of *respect*.

If you end up costing yourself the trust and/or the respect of a loved one through cheating, lying, addiction, or financial irresponsibility, then you better make sure you do everything you can to win that trust and respect back. Otherwise, it's pretty much guaranteed you will have sabotaged that relationship, temporarily if not permanently.

Specific Strategies for Sabotaging Significant Personal Relationships

Assume there are two possible reasons why someone may go ahead and sabotage an important personal relationship in their lives. Possibility number one is that your inner bully has convinced you that you don't deserve to have a relationship with your significant other. Unfortunately, these are your true feelings inside especially if you believe your significant other is in essence "too good" for you. This ultimately negative, self-deprecating belief can be based on the perception you have of your significant other as a person possessing very appealing qualities, for example, having a great personality, being physically attractive, or being very intelligent.

However, accompanying that kind of perception of your love interest can be the core belief that you therefore are not good enough for your significant other because you see yourself as having pretty much the opposite qualities that appeal to him/

her. As a result, your inner bully can convince you that you basically are undesirable to your love interest, and therefore if you have the option, it's time to get out of the relationship before your significant other rejects you.

The other possible reason for sabotaging an important relationship in your life is that deep down you do in fact really want out of the relationship! Your problem is that you don't have the courage to make that happen, be it in either a respectfully, tactful, and sensitive manner or in an ultimately disrespectful "hit-and-run" way. In order to actually extricate yourself from the relationship, you end up doing things consciously or subconsciously that are likely to push your significant other away and leave your love interest with the realization that he/she is not going to tolerate your sabotaging behaviors any longer. Now suppose your significant other in fact wants out of the relationship. That decision will likely leave you feeling less guilty about rejecting or abandoning your partner than if you are the one who ended the relationship.

It seems like a win-win situation, right? Wrong! If you end up terminating a relationship in a relationship-sabotaging manner, you have to deal with a virtually inevitable psychological trade-off. Meaning? On the one hand, you do end up extricating yourself from the relationship. On the other hand, by leaving in an essentially cowardly way, you will in the process lose some respect for yourself. Of course, if getting out of the relationship is all that really matters to you by this point, then any loss of self-Respect you might experience will take a backseat to the sense of relief you obtained by the exit.

When your inner bully causes you to sabotage an important relationship in your life, it will utilize the many "weapons" it has in its arsenal. Following is a list some of those weapons.

Betrayal

As discussed at length above, one "easy" strategy for potentially creating a big loss of trust in and respect for you is to do something to betray your significant other. Go ahead and, for example, commit adultery, exhibit a pattern of lying, make plans about your ambition and goals but not follow through on them, show you have a bad temper, or engage in some type of substance abuse. Do one or more of these things and you can bet the house you will sabotage this relationship. At that point, your inner bully is fully in charge of the sabotage, no matter how much you may really want to maintain this relationship. As always, when under the sabotaging influence of your inner bully, you lose and it wins.

If you can convince your significant other of your sincere remorse for betraying him/her and then make a concerted effort to try to make it up to him/her, then perhaps you will eventually be forgiven and your relationship "wound" will heal. That possibility hinges on your betrayed love interest having a truly forgiving heart and a tolerant soul, not to mention an inner core of some pretty solid self-worth.

However, let's suppose your betrayed significant other has pretty *low* self-worth at the core. If that's the case, then he/she may lack the courage to end the relationship with you. In that situation, you might still end up with an intact relationship after all. The caveat here is that bad feelings on your betrayed love interest's part can fester over time. If that is in fact what occurs, you can never rule out that he/she may *eventually* muster up the courage to put the kibosh on the relationship. That's especially likely if your significant other's self-worth eventually ends up on solid ground.

Hanging Around Too Long

Over the years, I've heard enough people in my office and personal life proclaim, "Geez, what's wrong with me? I keep choosing the wrong person!" One day, Betty, a patient of mine, was talking about this very frustrating fact of life for her. In fact, Betty was talking about how her "wrong choices" were a longstanding pattern. Suddenly, though, after a pensive moment in silence, Betty suddenly blurted out, "Wait a minute, Doc. I just realized something. If I'm really going to be honest with myself here, the problem is not that I make wrong choices from the start. It really hit me that the issue really is that I keep choosing to *stay* with the person; and that's even when I see all the signs that I should have gotten the heck out sooner!" I thanked Betty for sharing that major insight with me because I knew that in that spontaneous moment, Betty had hit the nail squarely on the head.

When you first meet someone you like, you are mainly if not only seeing appealing things about them. It could be a warm smile, terrific personality, great sense of humor, a way of paying special attention to you, intelligence, or physical attractiveness. Focusing on appealing traits or qualities like these is a prime example of what is known in the psychological arena as the "halo" effect. This means you basically throw both logic and caution to the wind and see the person as virtually "angelic," as though he/she can do almost nothing wrong.

Yet here's where some serious bubble-bursting can occur. Let's assume you have a terrific first impression of someone you've begun to date. It might already get you wondering something like "Could this be the Mr./Ms. Right I've been searching for all these years?" You make the choice to dive right in, head first, with lots of excitement that this could really be a great situation for you.

Here's my question to you. Even if the two of you have only gone out a couple of times, do you already have some evidence that you could be making a wrong decision to move forward with the relationship? If the answer is no, please nonetheless keep the word "evidence" in mind when you think about the fact that your inner bully has steered you into a pattern of making wrong choices. At the same time, if you have no clear evidence early on that you are making a bad choice, well, you might as well proceed while keeping your "radar" up for evidence to the contrary.

On the other hand, let's suppose you *get* some evidence early on that this person is really not all you've cranked them up to be in your mind and heart. Allow me to give a name to that evidence: *dark side*, which can be defined as anything you discover about this individual that is hard for you to tolerate. Feel free to replace the words "dark side" with the words "red flag," whichever you'd prefer, as the two sets of words basically are interchangeable.

Before offering some examples of the "dark side" of a person, keep in mind that the perception of what constitutes a "dark side" of someone fits under the heading of "different strokes for different folks." That means if you define a certain quality or trait in your significant other as a "dark side" of him/her, that doesn't mean the person will *agree* with you that it's a dark side.

As for some examples of "dark sides," there's a long list of possibilities that still do not exhaust the potential list overall. Let's start with these: a bad temper, a pattern of infidelity, a pattern of lying, a lack of self-discipline, a lack of ambition and drive, a pattern of being overcritical and undercrediting, substance abuse, excessive use of sarcasm, bitterness, social avoidance, cockiness and arrogance, a lack of compassion or remorse, few if any close friends, "skeletons" in their closet, a lack of verbal or physical affection, too much passivity or overaggressiveness on the sexual front, core immaturity, a lack of the ability to truly be romantic, or a pattern of procrastination and self-defeating perfectionism. Like I said, that still does not exhaust the list of the possible dark sides someone you are drawn to may have.

Now let's bring the inner bully back into the picture. Even when evidence starts mounting up about your new person having one or more dark sides, certainly one possible direction in which your inner bully can lead you can at best be called *downplaying* of those sides and at worst be called outright *denial* of them. As a result of either chosen direction, you may end up staying in the relationship a lot longer than you ever would have imagined! You choose to tolerate a person's dark side(s) in spite of how psychologically harmful you know on some level it is. In the process, you end up throwing caution to the wind as you continue to stay with your new person, maybe not till death do you part, but certainly long enough for you to experience a whole lot of turmoil in the relationship as well as internally.

Now at this point you may be wondering something along the lines of "Why would someone stay in a relationship when they realize early on that their love interest has some truly unappealing dark sides?" My answer to your question hinges in part on the answer to another question. If you are being totally honest with yourself, do you find the person's dark sides to basically be tolerable, barely tolerable, or outright intolerable? If your answer is *not* number three, then chances are you can and will stay in the relationship indefinitely with a basically manageable level of core agitation inside you if the dark sides are tolerable, and a slightly manageable but not overwhelming level of churning if the dark sides are barely tolerable.

If your answer is "outright intolerable," yet you choose to stay anyway, you know the chances are certain people in your life will tell you "You're crazy for staying with him (or her)!" However, what those same people have to face here is that no matter how much it can appear that you are out there in la-la land for staying, you have chosen to stay in the relationship for whatever needs of yours are as you see it actually being met. That said, it is nonetheless likely that the basis for your choice is one or more of the following reasons: you have low self-Worth, you dread the thought of living and/or being alone, there is a major financial problem that could develop if you exit, there are kids involved, or you feel very guilty about the prospect of hurting your significant other by abandoning him/her.

When you have reached that point, the moral of the story basically becomes no matter how intolerable any of your significant other's dark sides may be for you and no matter how much angst gets churned up inside you related to that, you choose to stay anyway. Additionally, you stay no matter how much you may bemoan that fact by over and over declaring "I really know I should leave once and for all!" and no matter how much everyone else believes you are simply *rationalizing* your decision to stay. This leads to the larger moral of the story here. Your "wrong decision" is not about your choice of the person to get involved with in the first place but rather, as my patient Betty realized, your wrong decision is in choosing to *stay* with that person anyway no matter how many of their dark sides may be hitting you squarely in the face!

When you reach this point, you need to be clear that the ultimate victory of your self-sabotaging inner bully is the negative feelings about yourself that will accompany your staying in the relationship. You are virtually guaranteed to end up feeling many more bad feelings about yourself than good ones. When you choose to stay, only to discover later that you allowed yourself to be badly fooled by your significant other, you can end up with some deep-rooted self-doubts and loss of self-confidence regarding your future relationship-related decisions. By keeping you in prolonged denial and therefore basically immobilized in the relationship, your inner bully makes sure you don't muster up the courage to get out of the relationship when nearly every indication is that you really ought to do that. This virtually guarantees that your core self-Worth will take another hit.

Getting Your Radar Up for "Charmers"

Let me now tell you a bit about a specific type of dark-side-ridden person, the type that can connect deeply to your problem of staying too long in a relationship. My experience is that this is especially true for you ladies out there more often than men, although both genders are in the end equally vulnerable to this type of person.

I'm sure you know the type: a guy with a smile that can light up a room, with a way of speaking to you and looking at you like you are the prettiest, sexiest, most enjoyable, and most stimulating woman on the planet, and with a virtually bottomless well of ways to make you feel how special you are to him. All of this is accompanied by giving you frequent, thoughtful, and expensive material gifts, compliments, and laughs like you haven't had in a long time. All of this adds up to what certainly can be irresistible charm on the charmer's part with, more often than not, the cockiness of the proverbial "bad boy" type thrown into the mix.

That's pretty much the dictionary definition of a charmer, wouldn't you agree? You don't need me to tell you that charmers are out there in the world. They are quite capable of making you feel like you've just possibly met your true "Prince

Charming" rather than merely just some charming guy. In the process, they are boosting your previously sagging ego. At the same time, you can assume that the charmer's ego is being self-servingly stroked every bit as much as yours. After all, you are his "prize," aren't you?

I want to emphasize here that a charmer's sway over you can transcend your intelligence, your accomplishments in your life, your ordinarily clear sense of what is right and wrong for you, and your ordinarily high level of regard for the opinions of people who know you well and whose opinions and judgments you usually respect. Most charmers can have a lot of power over you, although that power is one that you *allow* that charmer to have!

Several years ago, a colleague of mine and I decided to write an article about charmers. We based the article on the many stories about charmers we both have heard over the years in our offices and personal lives. The title of the article is "Charmers: Beware of Their Dark Side."

The gist of the article is that if you have a charmer on your hands, you owe it to yourself to be mindful of two things related to charmers and their dark sides. First, be conscious of the difference between someone being charm*ing* and a true charm*er*. Someone who is charm*ing* can have very appealing qualities while still being a truly respectable and essentially good person at the core. A charm*er*, in contrast, is someone who exudes charm but who simultaneously is either a narcissist or an outright sociopath.

For any of you who may not be clear on the distinction, a narcissist is someone who is extremely self-centered whereas a sociopath is not just a narcissist but someone who basically has little if any conscience at the core. On the latter front, keep in mind that a sociopathic charmer may very well have a specific dark side, involving manipulating you *financially*. The result usually is you end up giving him a good deal of money over time, which he never actually repays.

The second thing to keep in mind is how much your inner bully basks in its glow of diabolical glee whenever you end up being badly fooled by a charmer, someone you belatedly and aggravatingly discover really could not care less if he hurts you in the end. You're left dealing with the fact that by choosing to have stayed with a charmer for as long you did, you likely sabotaged not only your pursuit of true happiness, but your self-Worth as well.

I encourage you to do yourself two big favors. First, when you see any red flags or dark sides rearing their heads, get your "tolerance antenna" up and ready. That means you need to be totally honest with yourself about seeing any personal qualities and/or behaviors in the charmer that say, "Whoa girl. Step back a bit and don't get sucked in here because this guy could be trouble!" Second, if you do want to throw caution to the wind and go through an excitingly rebellious phase you want or need in your life, then don't worry a whole lot if you get burned by a charmer in the end. If your self-worth is in a good enough place so that the prospect of getting hurt truly matters to you, then make sure to go ahead ASAP and do some burning. In this case, go ahead and "burn bridges" and get the heck out of the relationship! Even if it leaves you with a genuine sense of loss, no longer being fooled by a charmer means a big victory for you via a rebuilding of your self-respect.

Creating the "Death of Hope" and the "Birth of Hope"

What follows is relevant not only to being in a relationship with a charmer but also to being in *any* type of relationship with a significant other who has some dark sides that are hard to tolerate. When it comes to that person's dark sides, suppose you continue to hope and wish that he/she will change so those dark sides disappear or at least stay holed up inside somewhere. From my perspective, the reality in both cases is that sooner or later, you owe it to yourself to come to grips with the fact that you have accumulated enough evidence to realize that your hope and wish here simply and unfortunately has no chance of coming true. To put it a bit differently, you must take that hope and that wish for the person to change and once and for all lay them to rest, that is, make them *die!*

I hope it's clear what the benefit of this death of hope creates. Specifically, it can free you up to have many more *realistic expectations* about the other person. For example, suppose you hope and wish your love interest will become more outgoing, less loud and boisterous, more courageous or ambitious, or less moody. Once again, let me emphasize that if your evidence is that the chances of any of those changes actually happening are virtually nil, then it's time to face the music even if you don't like how that music sounds and what it makes you feel. Then you can proceed to make a clearer choice, which may well end up being a more courageous, self-promoting choice, and stop waiting for the person to change.

After that, you can start committing yourself to either of two options. On the one hand, see if you can gradually tolerate the person's dark sides better than you have been able to do to this point. If so, then lo and behold, if you two work at it together, then slowly but surely you could feel the relationship being "reborn" into a healthier relationship. On the other hand, if you know you will never be able to tolerate the dark sides, then you know the relationship is dead, so go ahead and bury it once and for all.

Either direction you choose though, you end up with the opposite of the death of hope, and that's what I like to call the *birth* of hope!

One postscript though. When you force yourself to let go of the hope for change in a loved one, you may very well end up feeling a sense of grief. Although it may be in your best interest in the long run to give up this hope, you can still feel truly *sad* about letting go of this hope for change. At the same time, though, you know in your heart that you have to do this or else you will continue to be very disappointed and frustrated when your significant other does not change much if at all. Meanwhile, you need to be clear that it's perfectly *human* to feel sad like this whether you tell anyone else about your grief or not. At the same time, you can now remind yourself of a potential for a hope "re-birth," with more realistic expectations as the basis for it.

Challenging Relationship-Sabotaging "Unspoken Pacts"

In any relationship, you can assume there are certain unstated understandings about how things work. For example, on a superficial level, it is my experience that when a couple goes somewhere in the car, it is highly likely that the man will drive. Nothing in the discussion of relationship expectations and rules (e.g., to my knowledge including in the book *The Rules* by Ellen Fein and Sherrie Schneider) makes any reference to who will drive when together in a car when no physical reason dictates "shifting gears" on that front. It just happens automatically. Many other superficial unstated or unspoken pacts can be in place in a relationship as well, from who sleeps on which side of bed, to who sits where at the dinner table, to anything else that basically involves events occurring on an unspoken or assumed basis in the natural course of a relationship.

Sometimes, these unspoken pacts can be psychologically toxic to one or more members of the relationship. A prime example of this is in a marriage or in a family where one member has a serious psychological problem such as an addiction. In this situation, it is easy to believe that the addict is the problem in the relationship. After all, that person *does* have a very real problem, right?

The chances are though there are other problems involved here as well. For example, other family members may be suffering from depression, generalized anxiety, bipolar disorder, post-traumatic stress disorder, or even their own hidden addiction of some type. Difficulties within the relationship or family itself are also generally present. However, the unspoken pact in these situations is that those are not the "real" problems. The real problem is implicitly defined as the addict and their addiction.

Why is one person defined as "the" problem more than anyone else? When family members define the addict as the real problem, they get to avoid three things for as long as possible. First, they avoid having to look at any problems they may have and therefore their own need to seek professional help. Second, they avoid accepting any responsibility for contributing to the addiction. Third, they get to avoid addressing and resolving significant problems in the relationship itself.

Now who is really protecting whom here? Ironically, one could argue that subtly it's the addict subconsciously protecting the *others* from having to face any of the three things they really ought to be addressing. What would be the motive for the addict to take on this role of protector? It is likely to subconsciously be the paradox of loyalty. This "loyalty" is the unspoken pact that says *only the addict* is to be defined as "the" problem. By protecting the others in the relationship system, the addict essentially gives them a chance to "rally" together to focus a good deal of their attention onto the addict and off of themselves and the relationships.

What is the price, though, that the addict may pay for that "loyalty"? He/she will in all likelihood stay addicted indefinitely, until they manages to conquer their addiction regardless of what's psychologically happening for anyone else in the relationship. At that point, the addict's loyalty becomes first and foremost to *themselves,* which is where it belongs! This breaks the unspoken pact of loyalty to the other members of the relationship. This pact has an even more subtle agreement that says in so many words, "no one in the relationship is allowed to challenge any unspoken pacts of who gets defined as 'the' problem, especially not the person *defined* as the problem."

Actually though, there can be another basis for an unspoken agreement like this to remain in place for quite some time. This has to do with, in a sense, "punishment." More specifically, the addict may recognize on some level that another piece of the relationship's unspoken pact is an inherent threat to the addict of being "punished" in some way for *breaking* the pact--especially via the dreaded withdrawal of love and affection. That certainly would appear to be a schizophrenogenic, double-binding type of message, which makes it that much harder for the "problem person" here to remain on the path to self-loyalty. Apart from any issues related to addiction, I'm figuring the chances are you may recognize some of these unspoken pacts within any of your own relationships.

Assume that your inner bully has you convinced deep down of two related beliefs. Belief number one is that you are never allowed to see the truth behind these unspoken pacts. Complicating matters even more is the second belief: if you see through the pact and try to break out of it, you will be punished in some way, again, especially through rejection and withdrawal of love and affection. Clearly these are a pair of psychologically toxic beliefs for the member of the relationship defined as the problem. Put them together, and you end up with a version of Jack Nicholson's immortalized words near the end of the movie *A Few Good Men*: "You want the truth? You can't handle the truth!"

What I believe is the key to getting the courage to face the truth and eventually break these unspoken pacts is good old permission work! In this particular context, the goal for permission work is to slowly but surely give you the permission to believe you are *allowed* to break these pacts and their "echo" inside. Keep in mind that you must pursue getting that permission from someone outside of you because the inner bully has for a long time been telling you in so many words, "Hey, guess what? Don't even think about breaking any of these pacts or else you will have to answer to me!" As a result, as in any other situation where you are prohibited from self-permission, you must get it from your elected permission-giver, assuming you already have one in place; if not, you need to create one for yourself ASAP.

You must, however expect some repercussions from your permitted efforts to break the pact. For example, getting back to our pact-bound addict, we can certainly go under the assumption that this person is part of a dysfunctional family. Should he/ or she become committed to a path of sobriety, the addict's self-Respect will likely increase. On the other hand, the addict's recovery could become "bad news" for one or more other members of the family. Problems on the part of any member of the couple or family that have consistently been avoided or denied now come into focus. For example, if the addict lives at home (regardless of age), then his/her new self-respecting journey down "Sobriety Road" could force the addict's parents to have to face the fact that their marriage has been going downhill for quite some time. Now that the distraction of the addiction is fading into the sunset, the couple is left with the dreaded opportunity to focus much more on *their* own problems, which could result in the eventual breakup of the marriage.

On a positive note in contrast, suppose the couple decides it is time to work hard at rebuilding their marriage. Under those potentially quite productive and mutually beneficial circumstances, what may at first feel like bad news has the chance to eventually become good news if the work, especially via marriage counseling, ends up being successful. In turn, this success is quite beneficial for the psychological well-being of the addict as well.

Here's one more example of an unspoken pact that on the surface looks healthy and functional but at the core is quite the opposite. I personally know a family I nicknamed the Pollyannas, who always appear publicly to be one big happy family. There is lots of positivity with little arguing or quarreling except over small things like what's for dinner or what time they're going to head home. When I visit the Pollyannas in their home, they sact like the stereotypical all-American family.

Unfortunately, I know the actual truth for this family given my friendship with one of its members, who I will call Dan. As though hiding a highly guarded secret with national security implications, Dan recently took me into his confidence and confessed that all is not how it appears in his Pollyanna family. In fact, he confided that his sister had a bad case of obsessive-compulsive disorder, his father suffered from depression, and he himself was addicted to watching porn. Dan's mother is the dictionary definition of image-conscious in regard to the necessity for her and her family to appear to the world like everything is hunky-dory all around. At her unspoken insistence, the family upheld this Pollyanna-like pact. In the process, though, no real psychological problems were ever addressed, much less resolved. I must say that I had my suspicions all along that the Pollyannas were like a family version of the "emperor's new clothes" scenario.

From my perspective, the overall moral of the story here is that if you decide to break an important, unhealthy, unspoken pact in any of the relationships in your life, the goal then needs to become to make some healthy spoken pacts to replace the unhealthy, unspoken ones. More than anything, those pacts must boil down to replacing the "see no evil, hear no evil, speak no evil" pact with a spoken pact of addressing and resolving any signs of personal and emotional trouble that present themselves over time. If all members of the sabotaged relationship become willing to go along with that healthy pact, which becomes more likely if professional help is pursued, then the relationship will heal and grow, fortunately for everyone involved.

Depending on how long and how entrenched most unspoken pacts have been in place, turning them into spoken pacts is a lot easier said than done even with professional help. If ever patience was a virtue, this can feel like as big a challenge for it as any!

The "You Change First Syndrome"

Consider the following exchange between Dave and Sandra.

Dave: So let me ask you something, Sandra. What are you going to do about how big a mess this house is?

Sandra: Well, Dave, when are *you* going to take care of the garage and mow the lawn?

Dave: As long as we're going back and forth like this, Sandra, don't you think it's time you cut down on how much you're spending each month?

Sandra: Well, Dave, don't *you* think it's time to ask for a promotion at work?

Dave: So you want to play dirty here, Sandra? How's this? When are you going to lose weight like you keep saying you will but you never stick with it?

Sandra: You know what, Dave? How's this? I'll lose weight when you figure out how to romance me and make me feel attractive rather than just trying to jump my bones!

The dialogue captures the essence of what might be called the "you change first syndrome," or YCFS for short. This is the term I use to characterize mutually relationship-sabotaging power struggles between two people in any type of relationship. As probably is apparent from the antagonizing exchange between Dave and Sandra, the essence of the YCFS goes like this. Specifically, one of you directly or indirectly says to the other, "I'll change when you change first!" Almost inevitably, that declaration leads the other member of the relationship to announce, "No, I'll change when *you* change first!" These types of exchanges may go back and forth for many months if not years, covering a wide range of possible subjects, from monetary issues to domestic responsibility, to amount of time spent together versus apart to parenting, affection, and any other possibilities you can conjecture.

Typically, the communications involved in the YCFS conform to what I call "Newton's third law applied to human relationships mired in power struggles." Newton's third law states that every action produces an equal and opposite reaction. Applying Newton's law to the YCFS, you end up with this scenario: each time either of you tells the other person (directly or in so many words) "I'll change when you change first," it virtually guarantees the equal and opposite reaction of "No, I'll change when *you* change first!"

The YCFS can also be labeled an "addiction to winning." Specifically, each time you and your significant other stand your ground and refuse to change unless the other party changes first, you essentially are trying to convince each other that you are in the right about who needs to change and therefore they are in the wrong. This can be thought of as a shared, two-way *addiction*. Given the frequency and intensity of these exchanges occurring between you and your partner, it becomes a two-way addictive, spiteful-sounding pattern of mutually destructive communication, which takes control of both of you, just as you saw with Sandra and Dave. Your intelligence levels and the amount of love you profess for one another matters very little when it comes to this shared addiction. The only thing that does matter is that the YCFS is in control of you and your significant other rather than the two of you being in control of it.

If you really want to understand why a relationship-sabotaging pattern of this kind may remain in place for so long, it helps to look at what this syndrome is masking or blocking. You can assume that a wide range of vulnerable feelings that typically do not get addressed or resolved directly are behind the mask. These hurtful emotions can especially include feeling unloved, disrespected, neglected, abandoned, or rejected. These hard-to-face and hard-to-admit feelings that fester inside only end up as fuel for the YCFS, which is then channeled into the type of power struggles you witnessed between Dave and Sandra earlier. Nonetheless, these emotions must be acknowledged sooner or later by both of you, first to yourselves and then to each other, in order to get the YCFS under control at minimum and to get your relationship headed in a healthy direction at maximum. By acknowledging these feelings, you can then proceed to work together to address and resolve these issues once and for all. Then you and your partner stand a better chance of putting each of your individual relationship-sabotaging inner bullies in their place. You also then stand a much better chance as a "team" to gradually cut down on your two-way addiction to winning. I recommend that you seek professional help together with the goal of reaching a point of mutual *healing*, which counts even more than forgiving.

Play your cards right, and the healing can in turn lead to true mutual forgiveness, which certainly can help the two of you develop a more solid foundation than you may have ever had.

What's the "cure" for the YCFS? Let's assume for the moment that you and your partner decide it's time to address the masked feelings of vulnerability behind your addictive adherence to this syndrome. In doing so, you must commit together to cut down on *overprotecting* each other and yourselves individually from these feelings overwhelming you. As a result of this overprotection-related soul-searching process, you end up with a fighting chance to slowly but surely cut down on your relationship-sabotaging YCFS.

How do you put that theme into practice? I recommend that you and your significant other make a one-month commitment to replace your previous exchanges with an "*I'll* change first!" perspective. In other words, for that month, each of you will focus on being the person to change *first*, changing at least one thing you know antagonizes your partner. For example, if your significant other often tells you to lose weight and cut down on spending, for that next month you make a concerted effort to become more disciplined in those two areas. Keep in mind that you will make that effort whether or not your partner makes a change you want them to make, for example, help out more around the house or speak with the boss about a promotion. The same holds true in reverse. Your significant other should work on helping out more around the house and seeking a promotion regardless of whether or not *you* lose weight or cut down on spending.

By experimenting together with an "*I'll* change first!" approach, you and your partner can create a sorely needed relationship-rebuilding opportunity to go in a different direction regarding the relationship application of Newton's third law. Specifically, by working on changing your behavior first in some important area, you increase the odds that you will trigger an equal and opposite reaction from your partner. As a result, the chances inprove that he/she too will work on changing "first."

After the month has passed, both of you sit down together and do a monthly review. By then the chances are the tension between the two of you will have eased some on the YCFS front. If that's the case, then you have potentially two blessings. One is that you are working as a team to try to conquer your mutual addiction to winning. Second, on a deeper level, you are freeing yourselves up to help each other ultimately heal from your mutually masked vulnerable feelings. Once you reach that point, you can raise your hands together in victory over your respective inner bullies. These bullies will abhor the fact that the two of you are moving toward building a solid foundation based on the mutually loving and respectful expression of a version of "give and ye shall receive."

How Good Communications Can Happen to Good People

Everywhere you turn, you are bound to find books, articles, and talk shows that address improving communication skills in relationships. From academicians to "expert" pop figures like Dr. Phil and Dr. Laura, a whole lot of people in and out of the mental health field have weighed in on the subject of communication.

Many of these writings on healthy communication may be boiled down to a few main prescriptions. These prescriptions mainly include being more mutually mindful of differences in perception, the importance of timing, and what can be called the "three *C*'s" of good communication to be presented shortly. If you ask your partner to work with you to meet these communicative challenges, you increase the odds that your respective inner bullies will be rendered pretty "unbullyish." This increases the odds of the two of you ending up with relationship-strengthening gains and two-way sabotaging reductions.

Let's take a look at differences in perception first. Many years ago, a colleague of mine Michael Wegner and I published an article we called "A Couple's Dictionary." The basic point of the article is how people can take the same words and circumstances and end up perceiving them quite differently. This connects to one of my favorite branches of the field of communicational psychology: *psycholinguistics*. The latter basically refers to the psychological meaning of words and how, as in the sample dialogue below between John and Rose, the same word can have different psychological/emotional meaning to different people.

John: I thought you were kind of hard on my mother last night at the dinner gathering.

Rose: No I wasn't, John. Why do you say that?

John: Because quite a few times she said something you disagreed with and you got angry with her.

Rose: What? Got angry with her? That's not true at all, John. I admit I got kind of frustrated, but no way was I angry.

John: Well how about when you and she were talking about the best recipe for butternut squash soup? As soon as Mom told you she had learned the recipe from my grandmother, you got mad at her because it looked like you were offended that Mom didn't think your recipe was the right one. You raised your voice to her, which I thought was uncalled for, and that's not the first time this has happened.

Rose: Now hold on a minute here. Like I said, I admit I was a bit frustrated with her, but I absolutely did not raise my voice and I was definitely not mad or angry or whatever you're calling it!

John: So now you're yelling at me, Rose.

Rose: I'm not "yelling," John. I'm simply emphasizing to you that I was not angry with your mother. Just like I said, I was frustrated, not angry.

From my vantage point, there are two morals of the story here. The first is that John perceived Rose as being "angry" at his mother, whereas Rose perceived herself as being only "frustrated" with her. So our two loving protagonists here had different perceptions about the behavioral manifestation of the word "angry" as well as the word "yelling." Moral number two is what counts more. This concerns the issue *underlying* these differences in perception in the meaning of the words "angry" and "frustrated." From my perspective, the implied issue here is that John perceived Rose as being *out of control* of the negative emotions she communicated to his mother. Rose, on the other hand, perceived herself as being frustrated but definitely *in* control of herself and her emotions.

Taking that a step further, for couples like John and Rose, ongoing differences in perception like these can create the potential over time for a mutual sabotaging of the relationship. Once again, Newton's third law can apply here. Basically, one of you contends that "*My* perception is the right one!" which is virtually guaranteed to trigger the equal and opposite reaction, "No, *my* perception is the right one!" At this point, a communicational stalemate reigns, which over time can fester into big-time mutual resentment.

What do you and your partner do about these seemingly irresolvable differences in perceptions? First let me suggest what you *not* do. Frankly, I recommend you not do anything along the lines of what my mother would say to my father, that is, "I may not always be right, Charlie, but I'm never wrong!" Now admittedly she would on occasion say these words in a playful manner, which was actually pretty funny to me. Unfortunately for the most part, though, she typically meant these words in a much more serious than kidding manner.

As to what *you* might do then to attempt to resolve differences in perceptions, I especially recommend two things. First, remind yourself and your significant other how much your respective inner bullies want you to ignore the old adage that "the truth lies somewhere in between." Second, the two of you should commit to working on "agreeing to disagree" at times about your respective perspectives. When you are able to do these two things with some consistency—and therefore neither of you is the person who is "truly" right or wrong—you begin to go from communicational sabotage of your relationship to the solidification of it. Mutual respect—in this case for situational differences in perceptions—tends to do that over the long haul. The differences in perceptions between you and a significant other can go well beyond emotion-filled words and their implications. You and your partner can have differences in perceptions about a whole "shopping list" of subjects, for example, what is the "right" way to budget finances, the "right" frequency of time spent together versus time spent apart, or (if applicable) the "right" frequency of sexual relations. In each of these cases, the more significant the difference in perception as to what is "right"—or at least "good enough"—the more the relationship has a chance to be challenged and undermined.

That brings me to the next communicational challenge to keeping your relationship-sabotaging inner bully in check—the issue of communicational *timing*. What you and your significant other need to be mindful of is that just because you want to communicate something important does not guarantee that it is the right moment for him/her to hear it and communicate back with you. As frustrating as that reality may feel, keep in mind that at that moment, your partner may be in a bad mood, preoccupied with something else important to him/her, or physically under the weather. Under those circumstances, whichever person is feeling like it's not a good time to discuss an issue needs to be respected.

Respecting that need for space does not mean that you or your significant other reserves the right for hours if not days on end to hold off communicating. Instead, the two of you need to establish an agreement that if one of you feels the timing of the discuss is not right, then after a limited but needed "time-out," communication needs to be resumed as soon as possible. In the best of all worlds, the postponement of communication should never last more than twenty-four hours. The exception here would be when one of you is still semi-apoplectic or having a crying jag. In this case, you probably should wait a bit longer. I highly recommend that you never wait more than forty-eight hours, or else relationship-undermining festering and grudge holding can become entrenched.

Of course, there may be instances in which you or your partner may feel that the other person is simply being avoidant or manipulative by calling a communications time-out. For example, Harry tells Marsha, "Look, hon, I really need to talk to you about putting the house on the market once and for all." Marsha half-heartedly looks at Harry and offers him a proverbial, "Not right now, Harry. I've had a headache most of the day." However, Harry knows that when the topic of discussion is not something Marsha wishes to address, she will come up with some reason why it's just not the right time to discuss it. Harry perceives

Marsha as manipulative on the subject of the "right" time to discuss certain important topics.

What's the solution here on timing? Once again, if a timeout is called by one of you, both of you should agree to follow up on the avoided subject within forty-eight hours at most. Otherwise, accusations of avoidance by one partner are likely to be right on the money and avoidant behavior should not be deemed permissible.

Next on the communications agenda, we have the "three C's" of relationship-solidifying communicational strategies: constructiveness, compromise, and compassionate confrontation.

Constructiveness

Assume that your inner bully wants you to challenge your partner in *de*structive rather than *con*structive ways. In the process, your relationship-sabotaging inner bully can get you to be overcritical and judgmental of your significant other in a way that will only serve to hurt him/her. What can help here is to use what I like to call tactful/diplomatic "intros" when you or your partner want to challenge the other person about something. For example, suppose you feel like saying something confrontational like "You know what? It's hard for me to deal with you being argumentative so much of the time. All you do is make people upset with you, and that just pushes me away!" Rather than saying that, you might consider starting off by saying something like this: "look __, I know this may be hard for you to hear, but I really need you to hear me out on it nonetheless." You could also try something like "Please take this only as food for thought." Only after using tactful "intros" like these do you then present the challenge to your significant other's behavior. In most instances, "intros" like these increase the odds that what you want to get off your chest will be less defensively and more palatably received by that person compared to a more confrontational approach.

Compromising

If you ask your inner bully what *its* thoughts are on the subject of compromise, you can assume it will tell you in so many words, "Don't you dare compromise. That's giving in and that's really weak!" By being uncompromising and giving in to your inner bully, you end up with another example of winning the battle but losing the war. For example, suppose you tell your romantic partner that it is good enough for you to have sexual relations once a week. Suppose your significant other's response is to let you know that once a week is not enough and twice a week is preferable. Under these circumstances, if you're really going to practice compromise and not just preach it, the two of you need to agree to something like an alternating-week plan, that is, one week sexual relations occur once a week and the next week sexual relations happen twice a week. Assuming neither party for any reason strenuously objects to that approach, then the two of you have established a workable—not to mention pleasurable—compromise that is quite advisable if the two of you want your sexual relationship to be on as solid ground as possible.

Compassionate Confrontation

Over the years, I have marveled at scenes in movies or TV programs in which one person tries to shake up someone they care about by bluntly telling that person they are in some way, shape, or form messing up their lives. Examples might be a statement like "For God's sake, wake up and see what you are doing to yourself and the people who love you!" or "Stop trying to fool yourself into believing you don't have a problem. It couldn't be more obvious that you do. All I want is to be able to help you deal with it!"

I think you'd have to agree that these two statements are pretty confrontational, both in words and in tone. Yet I hope you can also sense the care and the compassion behind the words. To confront someone you really care about like this can take a great deal of courage too. That's especially true if you have a tendency to protect or *over*protect other people. After all, you don't want to hurt them, right?

Let me invite you to change your perspective on confronting people. Following from what was covered above on constructive communication, *compassionate* confrontation can initially hurt the person who is self-destructive. However, I will firmly argue that if you look at this type of confrontation from a "no pain, no *gain*" perspective, then you will become more willing and able to muster up the courage to do it. It will take getting another mantra going to become more confrontational in this way. In this case, the one I recommend most is "It's in *their* best interest, not just mine. It's in *their* best interest, not just mine!"

Once you believe this perspective and see that the person does not help himself/herself with any true effort and consistency, then how much courage comes to you will hinge mainly on keeping your *guilt* in check. In order for your guilt over hurting the other person to stay manageable, you must be mindful of the likely consequences of what would happen if you did *not* confront them, i.e., they will remain stuck in their self-destructiveness! When that is the case, you might want to make sure you aren't going to essentially be an enabler.

Are the chances good that compassionately confronting someone you care about will lead that person to really work on their problem? There are no guarantees, but consider this when your overprotective impulses take control: if you don't try that route, that person's problem will likely remain alive and kicking for who knows how much longer. Let the person get hurt and let him/her get angry at you too. Just know in your mind and heart that your sole purpose in bluntly confronting the person is to help change his/her life in a healthy and constructive direction.

Last but not least on the subject, here's a tip on how to compassionately—in this case I'll call it coax rather than confront—someone you care about who has difficulty expressing their feelings into being more able to do that when you ask them to. Assume for the moment you ask the person what they are feeling, and their response is a proverbial "I don't know!" So that you nor the person gets too frustrated by that uncertain response, you have two options to help both of you out here. Option number one is to ask the person to give a "yes" or a "no" when you ask them if they are feeling a specific feeling at a given moment. The feeling words could be any you believe the person is likely to be feeling at the moment, e.g., angry, hurt, sad, or discouraged. Going this route gives the person the opportunity to be guided into clarifying their feelings, something which chances are both of you will welcome.

Option two is especially useful for but not limited to dealing with kids who have difficulty dealing expressing feelings. Instead of presenting options for specific feeling words, ask the person if they are feeling "bad," "sad," or "mad." Sad and mad presumably are self-explanatory. "Bad" can mean either guilty, embarrassed, or hurt. These three options may not be as specific as you would prefer it to be, but it sure beats hearing "I don't know" don't you think?

Expectations

The next communicational issue that can be rife with relationship-sabotaging potential concerns *realistic versus unrealistic expectations* of each other. Take my patient Rob and his ailing mother, Marie, as an example of how complicated the issue of expectations can get. When I first saw Rob, he was emphatic in his belief that his mother was being "manipulative." In Rob's eyes, she wasn't as sick as she professed to be despite her doctor's diagnosis of degenerative osteoarthritis. Given that belief, Rob believed that his mother was perfectly capable of being more active, especially when it came to getting her housework done more regularly and spending more time with Rob as well as her two grandchildren. Rob's beliefs regarding his mother's "manipulation" convinced him that he was being realistic in expecting his mother to do more.

Now let's turn the tables. As Marie saw it, Rob had disappointed her in several ways over the years. For example, she felt that he never lived up to his potential to be a successful professional and bring in a very good income. In spite of this, Marie believed Rob could and should help her out more financially, knowing how challenged she was in this area in her life, not to mention how much she had helped *him* out when he was struggling through graduate school. Marie also resented the fact that Rob appeared to spend a lot more time visiting with his "loser" of a father from whom Marie was divorced than with her. Putting all of this together, Marie was convinced that it was a realistic expectation that Rob should show more loyalty to her than to his father.

What we had here was a pair of loving but frustrated and aggravated people in a parent/adult-child relationship, each of whom was convinced that the other person could do more and/or do things differently. The problem was that each person's expectation of the other person was viewed as unrealistic by the other party. Rob felt that his mother should have understood that he had had a bad year financially. He was therefore in no position to help her out right now except in a dire emergency. Similarly, Rob believed that his mother should have understood after all of these years that his father was a very lonely alcoholic who was dependent on Rob for a few hours of visiting each week. Rob's mother, on the other hand, had several close friends and family members to provide her with needed companionship. As a result, Rob felt he did not need to provide her with as much time and attention as his father.

In Marie's eyes, the issue was pretty black and white. Given the true intensity of her pain from arthritis, she could not possibly be as active at home or anywhere else for that matter as Rob insisted she be. In her eyes, Rob was being entirely unrealistic and therefore unreasonable in his expectations of her.

Not surprisingly under these circumstances, the relationship between Rob and his mother remained a strained one at best. Both very much wanted things to be better between them. Unfortunately, each remained convinced that his/her expectation of the other person was realistic and the other person's expectation was unrealistic. As a result, for many years, a stalemate reigned between them in which neither person wanted to compromise. If they had, it's likely that the compromise would have led to a chance to work on developing more realistic expectations of each other.

Fortunately, I was able to steer Rob and his mother toward compromise anyway. During a session in which both Rob and Marie were present, they were engaging in a few rounds of attack and counterattack. I suddenly began thinking about how much my father and I used to argue back and forth. In the final year of his life, we thankfully reconciled many of our differences and got along better than we probably ever had. With this insight in mind, I asked Rob and his mother, "What's the matter with the two of you? How do you know you'll both be alive in a week, a month, or a year? You don't know at this point. What you do know is that you love each other and want to get back to being close again, apparently like you were before the divorce!" Now that I had their attention, I implored them to help each other make their expectations more realistic via compromising. For example, Rob agreed to spend a little more time with his mother, and he hired a cleaning woman for her. Meanwhile, Marie decided to take about thirty minutes a day and push herself to do some light exercise. In addition, she decided to do some volunteer work, for a physically manageable number of hours per week at a local senior citizens center.

The moral of this story is that if you and your significant other want to get along better, then you have to do three things differently regarding your expectations of each other. First, you each have to be totally honest with yourselves about what your true expectations of your partner are. Second, you need to decide which of your expectations you believe are definitely realistic for the other person to meet. Third, you both need to stop *assuming* that he/she can meet those priority expectations without first discussing them together. Otherwise, you end up with how the word "assume" usually breaks down, i.e.,, the infamous "make an ass out of you and me." Instead, talk with each other openly and respectively about your frustrations and disappointment with each other. Then make a mutual commitment to work on meeting your significant other's realistic expectations more regularly while revising those expectations that are truly *un*realistic to meet. These two options are called compromise, the best antidote to the "plague" of prolonged, relationship-sabotaging, two-way, unrealistic expectations.

When Bad Arguments Happen to Good People

For those of you who are *Seinfeld* fans, you know all about Frank and Estelle Costanza. The Costanzas typically came at each other's throat without a moment's notice just about any time they were within one hundred inches of each other. The Costanzas were two bitter peas in a pod, a couple that probably stopped pushing each other's buttons only when they were sound asleep! They were a couple that arguably could also have starred in the movie *War of the Roses*—minus the physical insanity of that particular war story.

Closer to home, I can honestly say I grew up with a set of parents that I have often described as the "understudies" to the Costanzas. Just like the Costanzas, my parents were not bad people by any stretch. They just *acted* badly enough toward each other way too often, and for the alleged reason of the other person's "own good." In the process, they sabotaged their relationship in many ways; and yet in spite of that, they stayed with each other right to the end when my mother died first, to give credit where credit is fully due!

Getting an ingrained pattern of intense arguing back and forth between two people under control is a lot easier said than done. The combination of the YCFS and the misguided determination to not give in can over time become mutually addictive, enough so that it can feel like a "mission impossible" for the two of you to create a lasting truce, much less a truly peaceful and loving relationship.

How do the two of you work on getting control over your all-too-frequent battles? The key is for you to, as I strongly encouraged Rob and his mother Marie to do, face just how much you are *hurting* each other. Which you know in your heart is the exact opposite of what you want to do to each other. So the goal becomes realizing that if you could look inside the other person's heart and soul, you would see they have the same hurt inside that you do!

The other thing you and your significant other need to recognize about addictive arguing is the paradox that it at least keeps a *bond* going between you. In other words, maybe not consciously but deep down you both may feel that frequent arguing might be better than no arguing at all. That's true only if frequent arguing implies that you still both care about the relationship not going downhill. In contrast, a lack of arguing in a relationship that's already in trouble could mean *surrendering,* that is, losing the hope that the relationship will get better. This can especially take hold if there is little, if any, real joy, fun, or affection in the relationship as it now stands.

Assuming that the two of you finally get around to facing these issues together, I strongly encourage you to make a spoken pact that will need to be in place for a period of at least one month in order for it to have a real chance to work. You have to agree that both of you will do everyting you can to interrupt the arguing so that it can be controlled before it escalates even further.

The pact can be fulfilled in any one or more of three possible ways. The first is an old standard: call a time-out--which you could do in a non-verbal (and therefore likely less imposing) way, by signaling time-out like a sports referee. If you do so, it must be with the understanding that the time-out involves the two of you going your separate ways, preferably for a minimum of ten minutes. Separate ways means going into different rooms, going out for a walk, or getting in the car and taking a short drive.

However, problems occur with this strategy when one of you cannot tolerate the time apart even if it's brief. Exclamations like "Where are you going now?" or "See, you always run away when the going gets tough!" convey an intolerance that, ironically, may be hard for the person on the receiving end to tolerate. When that occurs, the chances of actually being able to take a mutually respected time-out are reduced at best and become a trigger for another argument at worst. A time-out strategy will only have a chance to work if both of you decide you want and need a time-out to help you control your *own* agitation.

The next two strategies for controlling a pattern of heated arguments are strategies that I assure you are not for everyone. If you and your partner can be open-minded, then I encourage you to consider either or both of these options. The first one involves either of you getting out some type of device to record the argument when you recognize that the argument is getting out of hand. Once the recording device is in hand, it immediately gets turned on to record, and it *stays* on for as long as the two of you keep arguing. Then, when you are done, you have to sit down and listen to and/or watch the recording together. The goal here is that by hearing or seeing *yourself* in action rather than concentrating on your partner's behavior, hopefully both of you will end up feeling embarrassed by how you sound in your *own* eyes. Better yet, if that happens, you might be able to share a laugh or two about it , with sheepish grins on both your faces.

It is very difficult to interrupt addictive, relationship-sabotaging arguing when in the middle of it. But if you try recording yourselves in action a few times, assuming both of you do in fact end up feeling embarrassed hearing and watching yourself, then you may be willing to use this strategy again in the future to help you try as a "team" to get some control over out-of-control arguing.

The other strategy I recommend is another old standard from the classic psychotherapy school of Gestalt theory and practice: the use of something like spongy Nerf bats or pillows. When the latest argument escalates, one of you gets two Nerf objects. Then it's time to basically smack away at each other one at a time, knowing that the pain inflicted is pretty minimal.. That way, you get to be "uncontrolled" as you physically "attack" your partner and vice versa, but overall, both of you still end up more in control of your arguing than when the verbal attacks and counterattacks fly back and forth. Hopefully, as with taping, you even end up getting a few laughs together in the process. You might want to consider a good old pillow fight as an alternative to Nerf batting if that's what suits your fancies.

These two techniques—recording and symbolically/playfully attacking—are not for every couple mired in episodes of uncontrolled arguing. I will say this, though: a sizeable number of major squabblers with whom I have worked over the years report getting their especially bad arguments under control more quickly when using strategies like these rather than less confrontational strategies. That's because you get to practice shifting from essentially being each other's outer bully to a toned-down and therefore more tolerable version of one. This in turn can allow the two of you to get some mutual respect back for each other rather than disrespect reigning supreme.

To put this back in *Seinfeld* terms, you and your partner want to work together to make a transition from essentially being Frank and Estelle Costanza into becoming the tamer duo of Mom and Pop Seinfeld. By no means do the two of you have to then try to progress from there into becoming Ozzie and Harriet Nelson. I'm sure you realize that's simply not doable, which is perfectly OK because life as a more moderately quarreling Seinfeld-type of partnership is still quite preferable for the health of that relationship than a Costanza-ish (or Archie Bunker-ish) partnership!

Chapter 9

Strategies for Preventing Sabotage in the Workplace

Jenna

Jenna is a forty-eight-year-old patient of mine who recently was hired at a midsized company that manufactures medical equipment. Prior to taking this position, Jenna had worked for eighteen years in a good job at another company, eventually working her way up to a middle-level management position. However, the work had become so unfulfilling to Jenna that she decided it was time to find a new job in spite of the great hours and benefits package she already had.

Then one day, Barry, Jenna's good friend, told her about an opening in a friend's company that Jenna was qualified to fill. Barry made it clear that he could "pull strings" and help Jenna get the job, which in fact Barry was able to do, much to Jenna's appreciation.

Unfortunately, though, within just three months, Jenna became convinced she had been misled about her specific job duties and responsibilities. Specifically, Jenna felt that the work did not tap into her skills and experience as a manager anywhere as much as she felt she had been led to believe it would. Because she had only been there three months, Jenna knew it would be premature for her to leave, especially since she had no other job lined up. As a result, Jenna felt trapped, much to her dismay.

Rather than "grinning and bearing it," Jenna proceeded to exhibit all of the following job-sabotaging actions: lateness, missing project deadlines, argumentativeness with her boss and coworkers, and being a mediocre "team player." All of these behaviors put Jenna's job in jeopardy.

From my perspective, there were two possible explanations for Jenna's job-sabotaging behavioral pattern. Possibility number one was that her inner bully convinced her that she didn't deserve to keep her job, given the irresponsible acts she engaged in as listed above. Under the circumstances, it became apparent that the "goal" of Jenna's inner bully was to keep Jenna on this job-sabotaging path and ultimately get her fired. Once her inner bully reached its goal, Jenna knew the result would be a loss of self-Respect, symptoms of depression, and difficulty in future job searches.

The second possible explanation for Jenna's job-sabotaging actions is more of a paradox. Deep down, Jenna believed she most certainly *did* deserve a better job. But given her lack of courage to actually pursue one, she basically allowed her inner bully to steer her to seeking another job by getting fired! While that was Jenna's ultimate goal, the downside was similar to that which occurred with the first possibility: Jenna would lose some self-Respect in the process. However, the difference was that if Jenna truly believed she deserved to get a better job, then she would likely recover fairly quickly after being fired, especially if she did things to rebuild her self-Respect. That way, if Jenna were to land a better job, she would feel more convinced at the core that she deserved it.

What could Jenna do to feel that she deserved getting a better job, and then make sure to pursue it as vigorously as possible? We came up with two main strategies for her to implement. The first was working on her self-discipline, especially regarding losing weight, as well as cutting down on the clutter that pervaded her condo like a "foreign massive blob," as Jenna described it. Jenna was clear that doing so would be a necessary ingredient for rebuilding her essentially sagging self-Worth.

The other strategy that Jenna pursued was committing to do everything right this time on the next job she landed, that is, regularly being on time, being a good team player, and never missing deadlines. Using this strategy, Jenna had a fighting chance to rebuild her temporarily diminished self-Respect that resulted from getting fired.

As for the outcome of this scenario, Jenna did in fact get fired from her job, which initially made her more depressed than relieved for getting fired rather than for getting the courage up to leave on her own terms. Yet within a couple of weeks, Jenna did some proverbial picking herself up by the bootstraps. For example, she became very self-disciplined about losing weight. She also decided to set a goal of thirty minutes to an hour a day working on uncluttering her residence and ended up doing a better-than-expected job of sticking with her goal most days of the week.

Over the next couple of months, Jenna did well losing weight and reducing clutter. As a result, Jenna did rebuild enough self-Respect to then actively seek a good job in her field. Lo and behold, within six weeks Jenna's courage in interviewing paid off for her in landing a highly desired job, much to her glee as well as to her newfound sense of deserving it.

What's the moral of the story here? When Jenna got fired, her inner bully won that round: but by the time she had ended up getting herself a sought-after new job, she felt that she had won the battle overall. This took a good deal of courage and determination on her part to pursue getting what she really wanted. I also gave Jenna full credit where I knew credit was due for standing up to her job-sabotaging inner bully and putting it in its place!

Going back to Jenna's original problem, another negative impact of Jenna's job-sabotaging behavior leading up to her being fired was to alienate herself from the people around her. Being late on a regular basis, missing deadlines, being argumentative, and not being much of a team player did not exactly endear Jenna to her bosses or for that matter to her coworkers. This by itself became a major source of distress for Jenna, given the fact that she is by nature an outgoing if not people-pleasing type of person, in both her work life and her personal life. Jenna knew that once she landed another job, she would have to do everything in her power to not risk alienating herself to her new bosses and coworkers while at the same time ensuring she was liked and respected as much as possible. This in turn meant that Jenna had to keep a stranglehold on her inner bully and not allow it to steer her right back down the path of sabotaging her new work relationships. She made it quite clear to me that she was confident that she would be doing that, "period end of quote!"

A Note On Workaholism

On the surface, workaholism may not look like self-sabotaging behavior because many workaholics tend to be very productive on the job, as well as dedicated, hard-working providers. However, if you look deeper, the chances are you will see someone who clearly is way overworking. No matter how productive any workaholic may appear to be, the workaholic is still engaging in some self-sabotage, particularly with regard to his/her personal life. Specifically, a workaholic can leave significant others in his/her life feeling neglected if not rejected. In addition, workaholism can be connected with *self*-neglect. Lastly, staying on a workaholism "treadmill" can keep the workaholic from facing his/her core emotional pain, especially feelings of loneliness, worthlessness, sense of failure, or any other distressing emotion.

Workaholism can be summed up as a "good news/bad news" situation. The good news is that a workaholic is likely to be a dedicated, hardworking, productive worker. The bad news is that he/she may be nowhere as happy in their personal life as they want to be.

Exercises

1) Make a list of any work-related sabotage you have committed over the years, especially the behaviors that led to your being let go from a job. Also indicate what feelings you had after losing the job. Were they feelings revolving around losing self-Respect, or did you have some feelings of relief?

2) For each of the situations you listed above, decide if your job loss was based more on believing that you deserved to lose the job for whatever reason, or for believing that you deserved a better job but couldn't muster up the courage to take the initiative to move on elsewhere.

3) Regarding workaholism, list any workaholics that you know. Is one of them you?

4) For each person on the previous list, what do you believe are the underlying feelings and/or circumstantial stressors steering the workaholic (consciously or subconsciously) to remain a workaholic?

Conclusion

Winning Your Inner Core Endurance Test

Webster's dictionary defines "endurance" as "remaining firm under suffering or misfortune without yielding." What I hope this book has made clear is that the tougher your self-sabotaging inner bully is, the tougher your "endurance test" will be in coping with and standing up to it. It can certainly be a lifelong endurance test especially if you've had to endure your share of *outer* bullies in different phases of your life as well.

Let's say you commit yourself to taking the "double dose" of prescriptions listed below for building up the courage and determination necessary to stand up to your inner bully's echoing "direct hits" and "sneak attacks" on a more consistent basis. "Dose" number one is heightened awareness and mindfulness of the role your inner bully plays in your emotional life and how it can create a whole lot of self-sabotage for you. Then you add in "dose" number two: utilizing the strategies presented in the final chapters to give you needed ammunition to stand up to your inner bully's never-ending quest to steer you down the path of one form of self-sabotage or another.

Put those two "doses" together, and I sincerely believe you will end up with a core feeling of being able to endure much more of what your inner bully throws your way compared to before you had read this book. Better yet, I hope you are now feeling more confident than you have ever been about how to get your inner bully to back off you once and for all! You may recall the immortalized words of the comic strip character Pogo, who declared, "We have met the enemy and he is us!" Well Pogo, it's time to revise your oft-quoted declaration to "We have met the enemy and he is our inner bully!"

My sincere hope is that as a result of having read this book, you will no longer think of yourself as your "own worst enemy" or that you "beat up" on yourself. I hope you slowly but surely start treating yourself like you treat your closest friends and favorite family members. By being more courageous, giving yourself credit where credit is due, having more fun, and comforting yourself when you need that comfort, you are cutting down on inner bully–triggered self-sabotage. This in turn can translate into treating yourself to potentially big gains in your self-confidence, self-fulfillment, and core self-Worth, much to the benefit of your overall psychological well-being. Always keep in mind though that this benefit will be met with a great deal of dismay by your inner bully.

The Importance of Dignity

When I was growing up, I remember different adults in my life making reference to how important it was to "look dignified" when out in public. Through many more years into adulthood than I care to admit, there were times when I had about as much dignity as any of my four beloved Seinfeld characters had, which was pretty much a big fat *zero*. The prime example of this was my bad temper when I lost at sports. You really could not look or sound any more undignified than I did, cursing and flailing around as though I was smitten by a particularly bad case of Tourette's syndrome. For me, having dignity in these instances could essentially be "mission impossible" as some of my closest sports buddies could readily confirm.

Fast-forwarding to the present, my perspective on dignity has evolved into the assumption that it has a tremendous amount of meaning in life. Specifically, showing dignity runs much deeper than the proverbial "stiff upper lip" notion. Much more importantly, dignity reflects maintaining *emotional self-control and composure* under duress, to the best of your ability and without going to the extreme of being a "stiff-upper-lipper." The more dignity you display on an ongoing basis, the more self-Respect you build up in this important area.

Something else though needs to be kept in mind about feeling and showing dignity. Specifically, it's pretty tough to show dignity when you are caught up in *entitlement* issues. That's especially the case for immature, bitter people who get caught up in what the world "owes" them for their pain and suffering. For example, if you are waiting for an apology for someone you feel owes you one but you don't get one, then you are likely to get and stay pretty angry. Meanwhile, you logically know you could either let the issue go until maybe it happens a second time or try to create a nonattacking dialogue. For example, on the latter front, you could say to the no-apologizer, " Hey, help me understand what's happening here. The way I look at it, you owe me an apology for _____. It's pretty clear, though, that you see it differently, so let's talk this out, OK?"

The moral of the story here is this: when you don't get what you feel entitled to get from someone, the opposite of dignity is likely going to happen. You will basically get agitated and either sound like you are charging forward into battle, or sulkingly retreat to the trenches. Dignity, on the other hand, means you either talk it out with the other person so it hopefully doesn't fester, or you get some internal perspective that helps you reach a point of being able to let the issue go. In self-Respect terms, that translates into the difference between entitlement issues undermining your self-Respect versus managing those issues so you *maintain* your self-respect. I don't need to tell you which of these two possibilities your inner bully very much prefers you do!

When you display dignity, you can still feel and display a wide range of human emotion, from excitement and joy on the positive side to anger and hurt on the negative side. You show that emotion, though, in a self-revealing way, but in the most composed and self-respecting manner possible. Recognize too that the goal here is not to demonstrate dignity all the time. That's simply not humanly possible. Instead, the goal is to be as mindful as you can be of how much maintaining dignity does for your self-Respect, the by-product from being respected by *others*.

So here we are, coming to a close, on this expose if you will of your inner bully. For one last time, I declare that for the sake of your core self-Worth and the important relationships in your life, stand up to that devilish troublemaker more than you ever have before! From my perspective, you really cannot achieve a bigger personal victory in life than that!

Last but not least before wrapping things up, what follows is sort of an epilogue to this book, that is, a set of postscripts titled "Some 'Foods for Thought.'" As you will see, these "foods" go far afield on topics directly or indirectly related to self-sabotage and the inner bully. I decided to include them because I hope you will find them to be additional useful persepectives on dealing with your inner bully.

Postscript

Some "Foods for Thought"

FOLLOWING ARE SOME RANDOM MUSINGS I have chosen to list as an addendum to what's spelled out in the nine chapters of this book. Some of these musings come directly from or were at least inspired by the words and insights of patients of mine over the years. Others came from various and sundry places, from readings, lectures, movies, discussions with friends or colleagues, to insights from God.

Koyaanisqatsi

About fifteen years ago, a friend of mine with a taste for the offbeat encouraged me to watch a strikingly unusual film called *Koyaanisqatsi* (pronounced "koy-on-is-CUT-see"). Directed in 1982 by Godfrey Reggio with music by minimalist composer Philip Glass, *Koyaanisqatsi* takes its name from the Hopi metaphoric term essentially meaning "a life out of balance." The term has fascinated me since the moment the film ended. Let me just forewarn you though. If you decide to actually watch the film, prepare to experience a pounding, nonstop display of video shot at fast-forward speed, accompanied by a pounding, nonstop audio of minimalistic piano music, with no words in it other than the frequent, haunting chants of the word "Koyaanisqatsi." Truthfully, it is quite difficult to sit through the whole eighty-plus minutes of it. But I plowed through nonetheless, in what I can only describe as an emotionally exhausting yet mesmerizing experience.

Here's how I have come to apply the term "Koyaanisqatsi" in everyday life. Many years after I saw the film, I was riding in my car one day when I suddenly was struck by an epiphany of sorts. What hit me in a stream of consciousness were some modern-life examples of forms of Koyaanisqatsi. Several of these in particular have undercurrents or manifestations of the inner bully.

Qualifications for becoming a parent

Think about it. In adult life, in order to be considered qualified to work in a particular type of employment, you will need an academic degree or training certificate/license in order to even be considered for the job. By the same token, adult responsibilities like driving a car and officially getting married require training in the first case and an appearance before the proper authorities to get a license in the second.

Now consider this. The single most important responsibilty in adult life, being a parent, requires *no* screening process, degree, certificate, or license of any type whatsoever! Regardless of your financial status, level of emotional maturity, intelligence, degree of available family support, and physical health, anyone who wants to be a parent and a spouse/partner has the nonnegotiable, God-given right to do so. When you look at this from the standpoint of logic and common sense though, you might begin to scratch your head and wonder: so how can you be a really good parent without any required training or counseling? Knowing too that your child's inner bully is biding its time inside, waiting for your kids to grow up to be vulnerable to its sabotaging influence. In other words, there's a lot at stake here, right?

Now the fact is, yes, you *can* still be a good parent, particularly if you've been blessed with a couple of role models of that ability. Nonetheless, from my perspective, if all lesser adult responsibilities require training but the biggest one doesn't, well, to me anyway that fact of life *itself* is a world out of balance! No, requiring parenting training doesn't *guarantee* you will be a better parent. But it at least increases the odds of that happening I figure, wouldn't you think?

The fact that there is no screening for becoming a spouse or parent will never change in anyone's lifetime. Further, there are instances in which someone who is very young, financially disadvantaged, emotionally immature, and/or physically limited can still end up doing quite well in the role of parent. Still, after enough years in professional practice, I know I speak for many of my colleagues who like myself have seen all too many instances of just how psychologically harmful it can be for children of parents who are maturationally and emotionally unprepared when entering into the world of parenting. It's simply a fact that circumstantial readiness entering into that world guarantees nothing about psychological/emotional readiness.

So if I had my way, everyone would be required to take a few classes and/or undergo some type of training in preparation for the realities and challenges of parenting and marriage/family life. To my knowledge, the only training that exists along the lines of a re-quirement is the process of Pre-Cana for members of the Catholic Church planning to marry and start a family. Even if Pre-Cana is strongly religiously-based/biased, well, at least it's something, right? Only then would an individual be permitted to receive a certificate or license indicating that this person is qualified to pursue those two monumentally important adult responsibilities.

R-E-S-P-E-C-T: Just a Little Bit at Least

In the past ten years, another brand of Koyaanisqatsi has come to permeate many families, spreading like a communicational and hierarchical virus. I'm referring to the reality of how many chil-dren of all ages treat their parents with an inexcusable degree of *disrespect*. From telling parents to "shut up," to using four-letter words, to threatening to call the local Youth and Family Service agency on a parent for completely unwarranted reasons, the hi-erarchy of parent-child authority has in too many instances es-sentially flipped. This flipping if you will is in my view a prime, family-life example of a world out of balance. It is one that cuts across cultural, socioeconomic, and ethnic groups. It is one that forces me to declare in a booming voice over this written loud-speaker you are reading, "Hey, you parents out there! If it's not already there, do whatever it takes to get the hierarchy of respect with your children back into its rightful place!"

As a parent, you may be wondering how you can take back your power. I want to offer you what many of we mental health practitioners call a "behavioral prescription." This prescription isn't a cure by any stretch; but it can help you manage the symptoms of parenting trouble spots. The prescription is based on much of what has been discussed in previous chapters as well as other writings and teachings on the subject of good parenting. It will be presented as a basic "Do Not List" and then a basic "Do List."

The "Do Not List" is simple. DO NOT in any way, shape, or form abuse, significantly neglect, or abandon your kids, *ever!* As seemingly obvious a warning like this may be to most people, in too many instances it can still manage to fall on deaf ears.

In contrast, DO provide your kids as much comfort, guidance, protection, affection (verbal and physical), truth-telling, encouragement, and discipline as possible. As another example of my liking to use acronyms, this one is CG-PATED. Frankly, it does not matter as much as some people may contend whether or not you were CG-PATED as much as you needed as a child. I will say though that if you did not receive these necessities, then that is truly sad, and I want you to know I am a hundred percent clear you absolutely deserved better. Still, if you are going to be the best, truly responsible parent you can be, then on behalf of your children, please make sure before becoming a parent that you get as much guidance and support as you can about good parenting. That's something you *owe* your children to get, so you can give them as much love and guidance as humanly possible no matter how deprived you may have been while growing up of these necessities. Or to put this slightly differently, no matter how much you may have grown up receiving nowhere enough CG-PATED yourself, try and do everything in your power to give plenty of "CG-PATED" to *your* kids!

You may be wondering how you can tell whether or not you are giving your child enough of the CG-PATED package.. You can start by looking for three main signs of potential trouble: 1) a decline in school performance, 2) a change in a negative direction regarding relationships with peers (i.e., either becoming overattached or self-isolating at home), and 3) childlike regressive behaviors. If you see problems in any of the three areas for at least a couple of weeks in a row, you can assume there's trouble brewing. At this point, you can either monitor your child's behavior closely for another couple of weeks or get him/her into a therapist's office ASAP. On the other hand, if you see no trouble in any of these three areas, then just assume there isn't any—fortunately. In fact, you can assume that you are giving your child enough of the love, attention, and guidance that every child needs. Allow me to offer you a very big "Way to go!" for that extremely important and well-deserved acknowledgment! Overall, adhering to these two behavioral prescriptions for what to do and not do can be a rock-solid antidote to the all-too-many instances of this type of Koyaanisqatsi of modern family life. In the process, it virtually guarantees you will a relatively tame inner bully in your child, something you no doubt would love to create for that child!

God Almighty: What Happened Here?

This next category of Koyaanisqatsi is the what I'm going to call the "good news/ bad news" of organized religion. Regardless of denomination or particular religion, it's safe to say that most organized religions share certain commonalities. One is a belief in a God, a supreme being, or a Higher Power. Most of them have an emphasis on prayer and some form of meditation. They also have a set of rules built for the most part around the Ten Commandments as a guide for human behavior. Most religions encourage members to love one another as brother and sister. All of that I think it's safe to say are the good rhings about religion—and I do mean *very good* things. Of course, there are major differences among organized religions regarding, for example, who God is, what He/She does, rituals, practices, and beliefs about the afterlife. But in the end, and at least as far as what they are intended to be and do for the people who follow them, I honestly view organized religions as–when practiced as I view God as preaching to all of us–truly a God-send!

Unfortunately, the history of the world demonstrates how many practitioners of organized religions have all too often *not* practiced what they preached. Without naming names, the history of the world has seen plenty of religion-based acts of prejudice, persecution, and genocidal wars done "in the name of God," while the other side is judged as essentially misguided at best and doomed sinners at worst. As a result the argument usually goes, those individuals must ultimately be converted to the "right" religion—i.e., theirs-- in order to be "enlightened" or "saved," and therefore remaining in God's good graces. In the process though, both sides in their prejudiced, self-justified, self-righteous quest rarely seem to step back and take a close look at how these often violent quests for "enlightenment" reflect in actual practice the complete *opposite* of what is preached! This may be why renowned German philosopher Karl Marx clearly was no a fan of organized religion when contending as he did that religion really is just an "opiate of the masses." Not in my eyes though Karl—it's really much better than that. When practiced in the intended way, organized religion gives people a greatly needed mix of comfort, courage, inner strength—and community too. From my perspective, that sounds a whole lot healthier a way to view organized religion than as a self-numbing "opiate."

Some people reading this may already be viewing me as somewhat to more than somewhat sacrilegious. At risk of only intensifying that viewpoint by speculating on what God's position is on the subject of religious people not practicing what they preach, I offer you following monologue about that position. Please be clear that what I'm about to present is *my* perspective and my perspective only. So if it appeals to you, great; if it in any way offends you, I understand if your belief on the subject is quite different.

From my perspective, God looks down at His people and sees a form of Koyaanisqatsi every day. In fact, I'm imagining that God has spent enough of His time over the millennia thinking something along the lines of the following:

"For My sake, what are you people doing? I do expect you to honor Me especially since I did create all of you, but do you really think that you are honoring Me by using my name to justify hating and killing each other? I don't think so! In fact, when I think about it, the term Koyaanisqatsi seems more appropriate than any other description. I never told you to create various organized religions as different ways to honor me. That was *your* well-intended but in the end disharmonizing creation, people, not Mine. In fact, I'll let all of you in on a little secret. If you had asked Me first before you created so many different religions, I would have strongly advised you to create a grand total of no more than three-- I'd rather call them--"spiritual" rather than religious options.

Option one would be one single organized religion honoring Me with rituals and practices that were created by a council of highly respected leaders of each religious community. Had you done that long ago, you could have saved all the trouble of figuring out which religious 'ism' you should practice by just calling it: 'God-ism.' I don't care if you call them churches, synagogues, mosques, or temples as to where to practice God-ism.. The only thing that matters to Me is that you show up to them once in a while!

Option number two would be these nonreligious, nondenominational spiritual centers and twelve-step programs I hear about, where there is no actual Bible or other book used as a guide for honoring Me. Instead, you honor Me in nontraditional ways that still show your devotion to Me. By eliminating the organized religion factor, it leaves you with less room to be so hostile and antagonistic toward each other.

Option three concerns those of you who are atheists. You may think I do not exist or have parted company because you feel that I have betrayed you in some way. Meanwhile, many religious people apparently believe that I am very upset with those of you who are atheists. They may even say that I am so angry with you that you might end up going to you-know-where if you don't get your act together during this lifetime.

In fact, here's the deal. What matters more to Me is how you treat each other, rather than whether or not you believe in Me or if you come to some sort of worship center. Even if you deny my existence, rest assured and you can assume I still have your back unless you abuse people. If that is the case, then you need to make amends, just like those who believe in Me do.

Last but not least, when it comes to deciding which organized religion is the right one or what rituals and practices are the best, you don't have the final say on the matter—*I* do. As far as I'm concerned, *all* religions, rituals, and practices are the right ones—again though, just as long as each is practiced in a way that allows all of you to treat each other with dignity and respect!"

There you have it. The paradox of organized religion is in its basically preaching a great way for the world to be in balance, yet in practice often ending up with a spiritual and psychological version of a world *out* of balance!

As a little postscript here, one day many years ago, a quite spiritual friend Kathy and I were driving out on some lovely country roads, listening to the timeless tunes of one of my favorite songwriters ever, Carole King. Eventually, on came her classic "You've Got a Friend." My friend and I began to sing along in a our typically loud yet strikingly off-key style, as we were transported back to too many years ago when we first heard her musical poetry. As soon as the song ended, my friend reached over, tugged at my arm, and with pure unadulterated glee exclaimed, "You know what just hit me Sidney? This song could really be about God! When you're down and troubled, you just call out My name and I'll be there. Now is that God or what?" All I could say to my friend about her welcomed piece of "schmaltz" was "I second the motion!" Yep, good old God, the Creator, the Higher Power, and, if you so believe, the "arch enemy" of the inner bully!

(I'm All for) Crying Out Loud!

It never ceases to amaze me how many people judge crying in public or even privately as a sign of weakness. Men who cry out loud are all-too-often judged as "unmanly," with the exception maybe of situations that can be emotionally devastating for anyone, such as funerals or destructive natural disasters. Under these three deeply painful life circumstances, virtually everyone gets permission to cry out loud.

It shouldn't take some form of extreme emotional or physical hardship to believe that it's perfectly *human* to cry, and to do so anywhere you darn well please! In her song "Court and Spark," another of my favorite singer/songwriters of all time Joni Mitchell says, "You know laughing and crying, it's the same release." Although both laughing and crying certainly are emotional releases, from my vantage point there are two main differences between them. First, I can't imagine anyone judging laughing to be a sign of "weakness" or "wimpiness." Second, laughing signals that we're truly enjoying ourselves whereas crying tells us we're really sad at the moment. Interestingly enough too, in the rare instances when you are crying "hysterically," what do you typically end up doing sooner or later? Laughing. By the same token, if you are laughing "hysterically," don't you usually end up in tears? Quite the paradoxical cycling, isn't it!

Lastly, did you ever hear anyone say they had a "bad" cry? I don't know about you, but I haven't. Also, if we aren't supposed to cry, then why did God give us tear ducts?

Enough said on crying.

Speaking of Manhood

Man, oh man, it's not easy to be a man. When I say that, I can imagine much of the female population calling out loud and clear, "Hey, it's not easy to be a woman either!" What I mainly mean here is that there seem to be two possible definitions of what constitutes a "real" man. This distinction has caused men a lot of trouble for a long time.

One possible definition is the stereotype of a proverbial "macho" man. There he is, physically strapping, emotionally collected, works well with his hands, very athletic, and sexually appealing. He is the epitome of the "Marlboro Man." Where does that leave the rest of the men who are not all of these things? Well, it leaves enough of us wondering at times if we are "real" men or not. We certainly aren't Marlboro men, that's for sure. Are we therefore not "real" men? No we're not, according to "macho" men and probably according to women who want and need a "macho" man. But I think there's still plenty of room for we non-machos to see ourselves as "real" men, and that goes for women who don't want or need a "macho" man in their life.

So here's any other possible definition of a "real" man. For starters, a "real" man is a man who above all else can respect himself for how he leads his life. That includes how he treats others, how dedicated he is at his job, what he is like as a parent and/or a caretaker, how he treats women, and how well he balances emotional self-control with human displays of emotional vulnerability. Chances are when all of these are done right, he will earn respect from others.

A "real" man is viewed as being a man filled with ambition and the determination and commitment to fulfill it. He's also a devoted family member, friend, and member of the community. Personally, it doesn't hurt one bit if he has a mix of qualities such as romantic, affectionate, physically fit, sensually sexual, and a good sense of humor. A "real" man couldn't care less if he's "macho" or not. In the end, all that really matters to a "real" man is that he is a man whom other "real" men and "real" women can personally respect and personally like!

As you know from a previous chapter, self-Respect has six components: effort, self-control, goals met, acts of compassion, acts of creativity and/or fun, and (best of all) acts of courage. If you think about it, aren't these pretty much the same qualities I just described for the definition of a "real" man? Therefore, you might conclude that a "real" man is someone who consistently does the six things on the Self-Credit list. In other words, a "real" man is a man whose priority in his life is gaining self-Respect as well as earning the respect of others.

The six categories of self-Respect can of course apply every bit as much to women as to men. In fact, you could say that both a "real" man and a "real" woman are of the same ilk in terms of developing this highly desirable quality. In other words, on the self-Respect front, gender matters zero! That fact of life renders both gender's inner bullies pretty powerless in the face of these definitions of real man and real woman.

Your Inner Bully Versus Your Inner Child

The notion of the "inner child" is one with which you're likely familiar. I'm imagining you are also likely to be familiar with recommended strategies for nurturing and comforting your inner child, as any devoted "parent" of their own personal inner child would do. Let me build on these by offering an additional recommendation for another way to take care of your inner child. In addition to providing it with a hefty dose of basic nurturing and comfort like affection, praise, and time together, help your inner child gather up the strength and courage to do whatever it takes to stand up to the very same inner bully that creates self-sabotaging trouble for *you*. After all, any inner child, real child, or real *adult* needs that balance for coping with life's bullies, right?

Being Reckless

One of the inner bully's favorite pastimes is to steer basically good people to do bad, reckless things. For example, it could be to engage in some type of illegal activity, abuse alcohol or other drugs, exhibit a pattern of pathological lying, engage in uncontrolled gambling or spending, drive recklessly, or practice frequent unsafe sex. These types of reckless behaviors can lead to trouble sooner or later in various areas of your life.

In spite of the potential for real trouble, though, the inner bully knows there are two main aspects to recklessness that can make it virtually addictive anyway: the excitement and the rebelliousness that can accompany the strong feeling of getting away with something. Reckless behavior is likely to create an adrenaline rush of excitement that keeps the particular reckless behavior alive and kicking for varying amounts of time. That's especially the case if you add on the feeling of rebelliousness that comes with not getting caught. In fact, given this adrenaline rush, you might say that reckless behavior can act like a nonmedicinal antidepressant!

Until the day comes when you finally get into some type of major trouble or you have the feeling that trouble is about to happen, your reckless behavior, much like any addiction, can remain in place for quite some time. That is exactly what the inner bully welcomes because as long as some type of reckless behavior remains in place, your inner bully knows that your self-Respect will be out the window. To top it all off, the inner bully is perfectly capable of keeping you from even *thinking* about what your recklessness is doing to that self-Respect.

Let's suppose that you finally do have some negative consequences as the result of your recklessness. Well, if you have a conscience, then you are probably experiencing a lot of guilt, one of the inner bully's favorite weapons to use against you. What can you do to get your guilt down to even a semimanageable level? Once again, it's the combination of personal penance and permission work to the rescue. The more conscience you have, the more guilt you will feel, and the more permission work and personal penance you will need to do. Otherwise, when depression sets back in, you can become quite vulnerable to the exciting lure of some type of reckless behavior again.

Who Are the True Heroes?

Recently, I was chatting with a friend's ten-year-old son, Alex, who is sharp as a tack. On impulse, I asked Alex who his heroes were. Out came three names: a high-profile professional athlete, a famous entertainer, and a character from a video game. I recognized that this was normal for a child of his age.

Then Alex turned the tables on me and asked who mine were. Since I could not recall the last time anyone had asked me that question, I was a bit taken back by his question and needed to put on my thinking cap before I answered. Then it hit me like a flash and out came my "quite mature" response. To the best of my recollection, I said, "Well, Alex, the people you mentioned were the same kind I'm sure I would have said when I was your age, but now that I'm older, the people I think of as heroes are people who do really good things that help other people. They do things that take courage and determination. A real hero never brags about the things that they do, which is what the word 'humble' means."

"Like who?" Alex unhesitatingly challenged me.

Pulling that thinking cap of mine farther down on my head, I told Alex, "My heroes are soldiers, police officers, firefighters, teachers, doctors, nurses, and all the parents of the world who do a great job raising their kids in a way that makes kids be as happy and healthy as they can be. But especially parents, Alex, especially parents!" Without saying it out loud to Alex, it then occurred to me as a postscript that real heroes tend to have either pretty tame inner bullies overall, or inner bullies that are rendered pretty timid during heroic acts. Anyway, on that note, Alex said, "Hey, man, that's cool," which made me feel like I was extremely cool myself, at least for that rare and brief moment anyway. We high-fived each other and went back to playing the video game in which his hero kept unabashedly killing a whole lot of bad guys!

So there you have them. A whole list of "foods for thought" related to and in various ways following from the two Parts of this book. I hope they added some insights and ponderings for you above and beyond all that was presented over the course of the main nine chapters.

I leave you now with two quotes. The first one is about *gratitude.* A little preface here first though. In a nutshell, the way I look at it, apart from feelings like courage, good self-Worth, and basic enjoyment of life, as big an "enemy" type of feeling to counter your inner bully is to have gratitude for, and therefore appreciation of, all the good things in your life. From your health, to your solid personal and work-related relationships, to your passions in life, gratitude is like an elixir to an inner-bullied soul. That said, I offer you my favorite quote about gratitude, by spiritual author Eileen Caddy: "gratitude helps you to expand and grow; (it) brings joy and laughter into your life, and into the lives of those around you."

The other quote is my favorite anti-inner-bully quote regarding inner strength and courage. The quote is from a Native American woman named Cecelia Fire Thunder, former president of the Ogala Sioux tribe. I found this quote at an exhibit in the National Museum of the American Indian in Washington, DC:

"When I think of fortitude, I think of internal strength, the ability to sustain no matter how hard life is. It takes a lot of courage to live in the world."

On that inspirational note, I say: Amen, Namaste, God bless, and signing off......

References

Barry, Dave. *Complete Guide to Guys*. Ballantine Books, 2000.

Bateson, Gregory; Jackson, Don; Haley, Jay; and Weakland, John. "Towards a Theory

of Schizophrenia." *Behavioral Science*, 1956, Vol. 1, 251–264.

Bradshaw, John. *Healing the Shame That Binds You*. HCI, 1988.

Braden, Darlene. *What Stops You? Overcoming Self-Sabotage, Personal and Professional*. Booksurge, 2006.

Cornyn-Selby, Alyce—Whats' Your Sabotage?; Beynch Press, 1990DiLiosa, Patty. *Taming Your Inner Tyrant*. 2011.

Dollard, John; and Miller, Neal. *Personality and Psychotherapy*. Yale University Press,

1963.

Fein, Ellen; and Schneider, Sherrie. *The Rules*. Warner Books, 2008.

Freyd, Jennifer. *Betrayal Trauma*. Harvard University Press, 1998.

Gibney, Paul. "The Double Bind Theory: Still Crazy-Making After All These Years." *Psychotherapy In Australia*, Vol. 12, No. 3, 2006.

Horney, Karen. *Neurosis and Human Growth*. Norton Books, 1950.

Hosseini, Khaled. *And the Mountains Echoed*. Riverhead Books, 2013.

Kopp, Sheldon. *If You Meet the Buddha on the Road, Kill Him!* Bantam Books, 1972.

Kushner, Harold. *When Bad Things Happen to Good People*. Avon Books, 1975.

Merton, Thomas. *No Man Is an Island*. Shambhala Press, 1995.

Newberg, Andrew (with Mark Waldman). *How God Changes the Brain*. Random

House, 2010.

Olweuus, Daniel. *Bullying Prevention Program*. Schoolwide Guide, 2010.

Poster, Stanley; and Hermes, Patricia. *The Self-Sabotage Cycle: Why We Repeat Behaviors That Create Hardship and Ruin Relationships*. Prager, 2006.

Seligman, Martin. *Helplessness*. W. H. Freeman, 1975.

Stone, Hal; and Stone, Sidra. *Embracing Your Inner Critic*. Harper/San Francisco, 1993.

Wormser, Leon. *Power of the Inner Judge*. Jason Aronson, 2000.

Made in the USA
San Bernardino, CA
31 May 2014